GREAT
PROPHECIES

OF

THE BIBLE

By

RALPH EDWARD WOODROW

In

Four Parts:

WILL THE RETURN OF CHRIST BE IN TWO STAGES?

THE GREAT TRIBULATION.

DANIEL'S SEVENTIETH WEEK.

THE ANTICHRIST.

GREAT PROPHECIES OF THE BIBLE

International Standard Book Number: 0-916938-02-6

A catalog of books and/or information
can be otained by contacting:

RALPH WOODROW
P.O. Box 21,
Palm Springs, CA 92263-0021

Toll-free Order/Message Line: (877) 664-1549
Fax: (760) 323-3982
Email: ralphwoodrow@earthlink.net
Website: www.ralphwoodrow.org

CONTENTS

INTRODUCTION

It is common, I suppose, for readers to by-pass introductions. It is our hope, however, that this brief introduction will be read; for without certain preliminary remarks in mind, it is possible some wrong conclusions might be formed.

There are four major areas of prophecy we will consider in this book: the Second Coming of Christ, the Great Tribulation (of Matthew 24), the Seventy Weeks of Daniel, and the Antichrist. Fine Christian people, whose sincerity we do not question, have often taken different sides as to the proper interpretation of these prophecies. In some cases, almost *opposite* beliefs are held.

Take the rapture, for example. All Christians generally believe that Christ will come again and believers will be caught up to meet the Lord in the air. But as to the *time* of the rapture (in relation to other events), there is not this general agreement. De Haan says that believers will be caught "up into heaven" *before* the tribulation period and that this "is the teaching of Revelation and *of the entire Bible.*"[1] On the other hand, Oswald Smith says: "There is not *a single verse in the Bible* that upholds the pre-tribulation theory....There is *no scripture* for a pre-tribulation rapture."[2]

According to Dake, the New Testament teaches *two* second comings: "The rapture is the first of the two comings....The rapture is the time Christ comes *for* the saints to take them to heaven. The Second Advent...is the time He comes from heaven *with* the saints, having raptured them at least seven years before."[3] Fletcher says: "*Nowhere* does the New Testament teach two future comings of Christ, first *for* his saints and then *with* his saints some seven years later."[4] Again we are confronted with two opposite statements!

Concerning the Antichrist, some say the Bible plainly teaches that the Antichrist will not be revealed until *after* the rapture.[5] Others say the Bible plainly teaches that the Antichrist will be revealed *before* the rapture takes place.[6]

And the differences do not stop here.

Concerning the seventieth week of Daniel, one side says it is yet *future*.[7] The other side teaches it has been *fulfilled*.[8] One side applies the seventieth week to the *Antichrist;* the other side to *Jesus Christ!*

With differences such as these, regardless of *which* side we take, we will have to disagree with someone! In disagreeing, however, it is not our intention to be disagreeable.

We want to present what we believe to be the correct interpretation in a way that is strong enough to justify its acceptance; yet in so doing, our motive is not to discredit those who may hold a different interpretation.

For the sake of clarity, we shall sometimes quote from various writers with whom we disagree. In doing this, it is not our purpose to cast any reflection upon their sincerity or calling. Though we may differ on some phase of prophecy, this should not be taken to mean there is disagreement on everything. The other person may have rich stores of knowledge on other Christian doctrines (which we ourselves may lack) and it would be foolish to say, "I have no need of thee" (cf. 1 Corinthians 12:21).

We ask that these things be kept in mind as the reader pursues the pages that follow.

—RALPH EDWARD WOODROW

Part One:

WILL THE RETURN OF CHRIST BE IN TWO STAGES?

We hear a lot today about the "rapture." It is preached and taught in positive terms on Christian radio and television programs. "The ultimate trip," as some call it, has been the theme of sensational movies. Bumper stickers carry slogans like: "In case of the Rapture, this vehicle will be unmanned," or "The Rapture: The only way to fly!"

Dramatic sermons tell how thousands of people will suddenly disappear into thin air. Cars will wreck, veer off the road, or plummet over cliffs, as drivers are raptured away. Planes will crash as Christian pilots go up in the rapture! Television programs will be interrupted as frantic voices give reports—a horrified husband says he and his wife were eating, when suddenly she disappeared right before his eyes. A mother reports seeing her baby instantly vanish from its crib. A Christian doctor who had just made

the incision for major surgery, suddenly disappeared through the ceiling of the operating room! While newspaper boys holler out headlines about "MILLIONS MISSING," church members (who missed the rapture!) will meet in emergency sessions, choosing new leadership, as they face the years ahead. The rapture has taken place! The trumpet of the Lord has sounded! And time continues on. *Is this the Biblical description of the rapture?*

One can search all the way through the Bible and he will never find the word "rapture." The word itself is from the Latin *rapere*, the same word from which "rape" comes—meaning to seize, to take away. It seems to us that a more appropriate expression would be to simply say what the Bible says: that believers will be "caught up" to meet the Lord in the air. Nevertheless, the word rapture is now in common use, it is applied to the catching up of believers to meet the Lord, and so we will not refrain from using it here.

The issue before us is not the *word* "rapture." The doctrine of the second coming of Christ, which has been the "blessed hope" (Titus 2:13) of the church over the centuries, is not the issue. That believers will actually be caught up to meet the Lord in the air is not the issue. The issue before us is whether this catching up (or rapture) is *a separate and earlier event from the coming of the Lord.*

Christians who hold what is called the "dispensational" interpretation of prophecy, teach that the second coming of Christ will be in two stages: first, the RAPTURE (his coming *for* the saints), and then later the REVELATION (his coming *with* the saints). The interval between these two events, the great tribulation period, is commonly regarded as seven years. Verses like Revelation 1:7, "Behold, he cometh with clouds; and every eye shall see him," are applied to the REVELATION—his coming in power and glory. The RAPTURE, on the other hand, is presented as a *quiet, invisible,* and *secret* coming. The following quotations are representative of this view:

> His appearance in the clouds will be veiled to the human eye and NO ONE WILL SEE HIM. He will slip in, slip out; move in to get His jewels and slip out as under the cover of night.[1]

Quickly and INVISIBLY, unperceived by the world, the Lord will come as a thief in the night and catch away His waiting saints.[2]

[The rapture] will be a SECRET appearing, and only the believers will know about it.[3]

In the Rapture, only the Christians see him—it's a mystery, a SECRET.[4]

It will be a SECRET rapture—QUIET, NOISELESS, sudden as the step of the thief in the night. All that the world will know will be that multitudes at once have gone.[5]

In all respect to fine Christian people who believe this way, to us this is a strange doctrine. The very text on which the catching up (or rapture) is based implies just the opposite!

For the Lord himself shall descend from heaven with a SHOUT, with the VOICE of the archangel, and with the TRUMP of God: and the dead in Christ shall rise first: then we which are alive and remain shall be caught up together with them in the clouds, to meet the Lord in the air (1 Thessalonians 4:16,17).

To us, this text indicates anything but a quiet, secret rapture. Amid the sound of the Lord himself descending from heaven with a shout, the voice of the archangel, and the trumpet of God, there will be the sounds of praise and rejoicing from vast multitudes of saints as they are caught up to meet the Lord!

Suppose the Bible said: "The Lord *invisibly* shall descend from heaven, *quietly.*" What would we say to someone who told us this means he will come visibly and loudly? Would we not brand this twisting of words as unsound doctrine? Well, then, turn it around. The Bible actually does say, "The Lord *himself* shall descend from heaven with a *shout.*" To read "invisible" or "quiet" into this description is just as unsound. If Paul was trying to describe a secret event, he chose the wrong words!

Jesus actually warned against the idea of secrecy in connection with his second coming: "If any man shall say unto you, Lo, here is Christ, or there; believe it not....If they shall say unto you...behold, he is in the *secret* chambers; believe it not. *For* as the lightning cometh out of the

3

east, and shineth unto the west, so shall also the coming of the Son of man be" (Matthew 24:23-27).

There is no indication anywhere in scripture that the second coming of Christ will be a secret event—only the *time* of the event is secret. Jesus stressed that men do not know the day or the hour of the second coming. It will be "as it was in the days of Noah" when people were eating, drinking, and getting married—not expecting destruction to fall. They "knew not UNTIL the flood came, and took them all away, so shall also the coming of the Son of man be" (Matthew 24:36-39). The wicked knew not until the flood came—but, obviously, when it came they knew it! It was no secret event. It was observed by believers and un-believers.

AS A THIEF IN THE NIGHT

"But know this," Jesus said, "if the good man of the house had known in what watch the *thief* would come, he would have watched, and would not have suffered his house to be broken up. Therefore be ye also ready: in such an hour as you think not the Son of man cometh" (Matthew 24:43,44). Christ's return will be like the coming of a thief in the sense we know not WHEN it will occur. There is nothing here to indicate a secret coming of Christ in which he will mysteriously take believers out of this world so that no one will know what happened to them or who took them. We should not think the Lord will prowl around like a thief, working in the dark, afraid of being discovered. The meaning is he will *come* "as a thief," not that he will *act* like a thief!

Scoffers will say, "Where is the promise of his coming?" But Peter assures us that the day of the Lord *will* come. We do not know *when*, however, for "the day of the Lord will come *as a thief in the night*" (2 Peter 3:10). But, again, the event itself will not be a quiet event, for Peter links it with a great noise! "The day of the Lord will come as a thief in the night; in the which the heavens shall pass away with a GREAT NOISE"!

In the noted rapture passage, after speaking of the Lord's coming with a shout, etc., Paul goes on to explain that we do not know *when* this will be, for that day will come as a thief in the night. "But of the times and seasons, brethren, you have no need that I write unto you. For yourselves know perfectly that the day of the Lord so cometh *as a thief in the night*" (1 Thessalonians 5:1,2). What is unknown and hidden? It cannot be that the coming of Christ, the event itself, will be secret. The context speaks of this as being glorious, open, noisy. It is the *time* that is unrevealed.

TRIUMPH IN TRIBULATION

Shortly before his death, Jesus spoke these words to his disciples: "In the world you shall have *tribulation*..." (John 16:33). The verses that follow record the prayer in which Jesus prayed for his disciples: "I pray *not* that thou shouldest *take them out of the world*, but that thou shouldest keep them from the evil" (John 17:15).

Though it would be no easy task to take a stand for Christ; though they would be persecuted; though in the world they would have tribulation; yet, Jesus did not pray that the church would be taken out of the world! The church was to remain *in* the world, but it would not be *of* the world.

Some might object, however, that Jesus was praying only for his immediate disciples of that time. But not so! "Neither pray I for these alone," he said, "but for them *also* which shall believe on me through their word" (verse 20). Does this not include us today? Have not we believed on Christ as a result of the message handed down to us from those original disciples? Indeed we have. So Jesus was praying for us too! He said so. He prayed we would be kept from the evil of the world, but he did not pray that we would be taken out of the world—even though in the world we would have tribulation!

Let us suppose Jesus had told believers: "In the world there shall be tribulation...but I will pray that you will be taken out of the world." If Jesus said this, those who teach a pre-tribulation rapture would have a basis for their position—and this statement would no doubt be quoted *often* as a proof text. But since this is *not* what the verse says—but just the *opposite*—surely this should be regarded as evidence against the idea of a special, "secret" coming of Christ to take the church out of this world.

5

Instead of the church being taken out of the world, Jesus taught that it would remain in the world to accomplish a definite purpose: to preach the gospel. Jesus commissioned his disciples to "go...and teach all nations" and promised: "Lo, I am with you alway, even unto the *end* of the world [*aion*—age]" (Matthew 28:19,20).

UNTIL THE END

How long would the church be in the world fulfilling this divine commission? The implication is that this mission would continue until the end of the age. Surely this promise would be strange if God's plan was to remove the church seven years *before* that time! If, when the end of the age comes, the church would no longer be on earth, a promise such as this would be meaningless.

Earlier in the book of Matthew, Jesus made the same point. He gave a parable about a man who sowed good seed in his field, but an enemy sowed tares among the wheat. When the crop had grown, and the servants discovered what had happened, they asked if they should pull up the tares. To this the owner replied: "Let both grow together until the harvest: and in the time of harvest I will say to the reapers, Gather together first the tares, and bind them in bundles to burn them: but gather the wheat into my barn" (Matthew 13:24-30).

We are not left to speculate as to the correct meaning of the parable, for Jesus explained. The good seed, the wheat, is sown by "the Son of man"—Jesus Christ. The tares, the children of the wicked one, are sown by the enemy—"the devil." They are sown in the same field—"the world"—where both grow together until the harvest. "The harvest is the end of the world" (verses 37-39).

"As therefore the tares are gathered and burned in the fire; so shall it be in *the end of this world.* The Son of man shall send forth his angels, and they shall gather out of his kingdom all things that offend, and them which do iniquity; and shall cast them into a furnace of fire....*Then* shall the righteous shine forth as the sun in the kingdom of their Father" (verses 40-43). Plainly, the time of separation between those which do iniquity and the righteous is at the *end!*

6

Jesus said that "BOTH" would grow "TOGETHER" until the "END OF THE WORLD"—and *then* would be the harvest, producing the great separation. This is the Bible teaching. But the pre-tribulation rapture position, to be consistent, would have to say that BOTH will NOT grow together in the field until the end of the world, for they teach the wheat will be harvested sooner, being separated from the tares seven years BEFORE the end!

According to a footnote in the *Scofield Reference Bible*, "At the end of this age (v. 40) the tares are set apart for burning, but *first* the wheat is gathered into the barn."[6] But if anything might be implied as coming "first," it would be the judgment upon the wicked, for in the parable portion it said: "Gather together FIRST the tares" for destruction, "but gather the wheat into my barn" (Matthew 13:30). What? The scripture says: "First the tares." The note in the Scofield Bible says just the opposite! Such twisting of terms does not speak well for the pre-tribulation view.

Looking further in Matthew 13, Jesus likened the kingdom to a net which was cast into the sea. It gathered fish of every kind—some good, and some bad. Finally, the good were placed into vessels and the bad were cast away. *When* would this great separation occur? "So shall it be at the END of the world: the angels shall come forth, and sever the wicked from among the just, and shall cast them into the furnace of fire" (Matthew 13:47-50).

Jesus further likened the time of his return to the days of Lot. "As it was in the days of Lot; they did eat, they drank, they bought, they sold, they planted, they builded"—those common, routine things that people have been doing all along, not expecting any catastrophe—"but the same day that Lot went out of Sodom it rained fire and brimstone from heaven, and destroyed them all. Even thus shall it be in the day when the Son of man is revealed" (Luke 17:28-30). Lot, the believer, was spared. The unbelievers were destroyed. So when Christ returns, believers will be spared (caught up to meet the Lord in the air!) while that "same day" fiery destruction shall fall upon the world. There is nothing in this passage to suggest Lot went out of Sodom and then seven years later the fiery destruction fell. These things happened the *same day.*

Jesus likened his second coming to the destruction of the flood in the days of Noah. "But as the days of Noah were, so shall also the coming of the Son of man be. For as in the days that were before the flood they were eating and drinking, marrying and giving in marriage...and knew not until the flood came, and took them all away ["destroyed them all"—Luke 17:27]. So shall also the coming of the Son of man be. Then shall two be in the field; the one shall be taken and the other left" (Matthew 24:37-42).

ONE TAKEN AND THE OTHER LEFT

Sermons have sometimes been preached about "one shall be TAKEN, and the other LEFT," as though this meant believers would be *taken* up in the rapture and the unbelievers would be *left* to go through the tribulation period. But this can hardly be correct, for in the context it was the unbelievers who were taken away—by the destruction of the flood. In the days of Noah, the unbelievers "knew not until the flood came, and TOOK *them* all away; *so* shall also the coming of the Son of man be. Then shall two be in the field; the one shall be TAKEN, and the other left. Two women shall be grinding at the mill; the one shall be TAKEN, and the other left" (Matthew 24:39-42).

If we understand this in the light of the context, it will be *unbelievers* who will be *taken*—in death, by the "sudden destruction" that will accompany the Lord when he comes (1 Thessalonians 5:3). Those who believe in Christ will be *left*—their lives spared. True, they will be spared by being caught up—up above the sudden destruction—but this does not seem to be the primary point here.

Though the world was formerly destroyed by water, it was pointed out by Peter that the destruction the world now faces will be by *fire*. "The world that then was, being overflowed with water, perished: but the heavens and the earth, which are now, by the same word are kept in store, reserved unto fire" (2 Peter 3:6,7).

Peter had personally heard Jesus give the promise: "I will come again, and receive you unto myself" (John 14:3). Years passed and some began to scoff at this promise, saying: "Where is the promise of his coming?" To this Peter replied: "The Lord is not slack concerning his promise...the day of the Lord *will* come...IN THE WHICH the heavens shall pass away with a great noise, and the elements shall melt with fervent heat, the earth also and the works that are therein shall be burned up...all these things shall be dissolved" (2 Peter 3:10,11). Thus did he describe what Jesus had called "the end of the world."

Some believe such statements refer to a literal end of this planet. Others believe that the end of the age, but not necessarily the end of the planet, is the correct meaning. In Noah's day, it is pointed out, "the world that then was...perished"—but the planet remained; so likewise, "the heavens and the earth which are now"—this age—could end and the planet remain. But, either way, "the end of the world" is the *end*—there is a distinct finality here. There is no indication or room for the idea that time will continue on for another seven years after this. We do not believe it was a bad choice of words when the hymn writer said: "When the trumpet of the Lord shall sound and *time shall be no more...*"

Peter continues: "Seeing then that all these things shall be dissolved, what manner of person ought you to be in all holy conversation and godliness. *Looking for* and hasting unto the coming of the day of God, wherein the heavens being on fire shall be dissolved, and the elements shall melt with fervent heat?" (verses 11,12). Obviously Peter did not believe Christians would be taken out of the world seven years before the end. Why would he exhort them to be "looking for" the coming of the day of God when the heavens shall pass away? Why talk of the *end*, if their real hope was an event seven years earlier?

According to Peter, "the coming of the Lord"—"the day of the Lord" which will come "as a thief in the night"—is the time when the heavens shall pass away and the earth shall melt with fervent heat. And according to Paul, "the day of the Lord" which will come "as a thief in the night" (the *same* expression) is the time of the rapture:

"The Lord himself shall descend from heaven...we which are alive and remain shall be caught up...in the clouds, to meet the Lord in the air....But of the times and seasons [when this shall happen], brethren, you have no need that I write unto you. For yourselves know perfectly

9

that the day of the Lord so cometh as a thief in the night. For when they shall say, Peace and safety; then sudden destruction cometh upon them, as travail upon a woman with child; and they shall not escape" (1 Thessalonians 4:16-5:3). This passage, even though it spans two chapters, is all connected together. There is not the slightest hint that the rapture is a separate event from the destruction that will befall the world at the end.

"HEAVEN AND EARTH SHALL PASS AWAY"

Jesus expressed the finality of that day in these words: "Heaven and earth shall pass away....But of that day and hour knoweth no man, no, not the angels of heaven, but my Father only....Watch therefore: for you know not what hour your Lord doth come" (Matthew 24:36-42). If believers are to "watch" for that day—when heaven and earth shall pass away—it is evident they were not to be taken away seven years before.

Even the ancient Job implied the resurrection would not take place until the heavens shall pass away. "Man dieth, and wasteth away: yea, man giveth up the ghost, and where is he?...Man lieth down, and riseth not: *till the heavens be no more*, they shall not awake, nor be raised out of their sleep" (Job 14:10-12; 19:26,27). Expressions such as "till the heavens be no more," "the heavens shall pass away with a great noise," "heaven and earth shall pass away," all seem to indicate the very end of things as we know them. Until that time, the dead shall not be resurrected.

Thus Martha believed Lazarus would "rise again in the resurrection AT THE LAST DAY" (John 11:24). This was not mere speculation on her part, for Jesus himself repeatedly spoke of the resurrection as being "AT THE LAST DAY" (John 6:39,40,44,54). Since the catching up or rapture occurs at the same time as the resurrection of the dead in Christ (1 Thessalonians 4:16,17), it is plain to see the rapture takes place at the last day, not seven years *before* the last day!

In the resurrection chapter (1 Corinthians 15), we are told that these things will occur "at the *last* trump: for the trumpet shall sound, and the dead shall be raised incorruptible, and we shall be changed" (verses 51,52). We know also, that on this "last day" at the "last trump," the "last enemy" shall be destroyed. Paul says "the last enemy that shall be destroyed is death" (1 Corinthians 15:26).

It will happen "in a moment, in the twinkling of an eye, at the last trump: for the trumpet shall sound, and the dead shall be raised...then"—at the resurrection and catching up—"*then* shall be brought to pass the saying that is written, Death is swallowed up in victory" (verses 52-54). According to dispensationalism, this happens before the tribulation—with seven years yet to go. But, then, what about people who will be killed after that, some of them being martyrs for Christ? The dispensational interpretation requires another resurrection at the end of the tribulation for them. Thus, if the last enemy is destroyed before the tribulation, it will have to be destroyed *again* after the tribulation! But put the destruction of the last enemy at the "last day," as the Bible does, and the last enemy is the *last* enemy!

What about tribulation martyrs? John saw people who refused to worship the beast and were beheaded. But "they lived and reigned with Christ a thousand years....*This is the first resurrection.* Blessed and holy is he that hath part in the first resurrection" (Revelation 20:4-6). Dispensationalism claims that these are people, martyred *after* the rapture of the church, who will be resurrected at the end of the tribulation period. But since the resurrection takes place at the rapture—as both sides agree—if the rapture takes place *before* the tribulation, how could a resurrection of tribulation martyrs be "the *first* resurrection"? On the other hand, if the "first resurrection" is a bodily resurrection before the tribulation, these tribulation martyrs would be raised from the dead *before they were martyred!* But place the resurrection at the END, as the Bible does, and a scriptural harmony is obtained. Regardless of how we interpret Revelation 20:4-6, or whether the martyrs lived in the beginning centuries, during the Dark Ages, or the final years of this age, with the resurrection at the end, all are included without artificial additions to the Word.

Until the rise of the secret rapture teaching (which is of comparatively recent origin), the idea of anyone being

11

saved AFTER the coming of the Lord would have been considered strange indeed! Did the church *ever* in the first eighteen centuries of its history teach such a thing? Faithful preachers over the centuries voiced what Jesus and the apostles taught—about being sober, ready, watching, waiting for the Lord's return. Peter regarded the seeming delay in the Lord's coming as God's "longsuffering," allowing men additional time to repent (2 Peter 3:9). Obviously he did not believe people would be saved *after* the coming of the Lord!

But with the escape rapture teaching, there is not that urgency. After all, if one misses the rapture, as it is now taught, he can still get saved! According to *The Late Great Planet Earth*, not only will people be saved after the rapture, but this will be *the greatest time of evangelism the earth has ever known!* "After the Christians are gone God is going to reveal himself in a special way to 144,000 physical, literal Jews who are going to believe with a vengeance that Jesus is the Messiah. They are going to be 144,000 Jewish Billy Grahams turned loose on this earth—the earth will never know a period of evangelism like this period....They are going to have the greatest number of converts in all history."[7]

Imagine that—multitudes of people getting saved *after* the coming of the Lord (the rapture)! We can only say, this has never been the Biblical or historical position of the church. But now, some churches have announced an addition to their bylaws: a legal notice passing on the leadership of the church to backsliders and sinners! These, it is believed, will repent and be saved *after* the Lord comes in the rapture. If any had doubts before about Christianity, with millions "missing," they will now know for sure! They are to gather for an emergency board meeting—these people who *missed the rapture*—to elect new leaders so the work of the church can continue.

A DIFFERENT PLAN OF SALVATION?

Some believe that after the pre-tribulation rapture, God will have a different plan of salvation! As one writer says, "Now we can be saved by the blood of Christ; but after the rapture, people will have to *give their own blood* to be saved—it will be a martyrs' route to heaven!" Another suggests that then people will be saved or lost on the basis of *how they treat the Jews.* A tract before me says: "If you should be left behind when Jesus comes...do not persecute the Jews...assist them in their distresses. For it may turn to be your salvation...those who have protected and cared for the Jews...who have hidden them, also fed and clothed them, will be found worthy of entrance into the kingdom age."

This concept is based, supposedly, on the words of Jesus in the parable of the sheep and the goats. To the righteous—the sheep—Jesus will state they fed him, gave him drink, took him in as a stranger, and visited him in prison. And they will ask when they saw him in these circumstances. His reply: "Inasmuch as you have done it unto one of the least of these MY BRETHREN, you have done it unto me" (Matthew 25:40).

The dispensational belief, that "my brethren" means Jews during the tribulation period, introduces a third class of people into the parable—in addition to the sheep and goats. This is not justified, for Jesus was not speaking of a separate class of people, but simply spoke to the sheep, the righteous, as "my brethren." It is no different than if he had said: "My brethren, because you did it unto the least of these—the hungry, the thirsty, the sick, the oppressed," etc. The proof for this is evident, for the word "brethren" *only* appears when Jesus was speaking to the sheep. When he spoke to the goats, the word "brethren" is absent, as the following parallel shows:

TO THE SHEEP	TO THE GOATS
"Inasmuch as you have done it unto one of the least of these MY BRETHREN, you have done it unto me" (Matthew 25:40).	"Inasmuch as you did it not to one of the least of these, you did it not to me" (Matthew 25:45).

Once the entire passage is read, the point will become obvious. If "my brethren" meant a separate class of people—rather than a simple form of address to those termed "sheep"—it should have appeared in the second portion also. Besides, Christ's "brethren" could hardly mean a group of Jews—in a *fleshly* sense—for Jesus himself said (as also recorded in Matthew) that *all* who do the will of the Father are his brethren (Matthew 12:48-50). It is a relationship based on GRACE, *not* RACE!

NO ONE KNOWS THE DAY OR HOUR

Over and over the Bible has stressed that the coming of the Lord will suddenly occur, that the time is unknown, that no man knows the day or hour of the end of the age. But if the rapture is an event to take place seven years *before* the end, *thousands* of people would be able to determine the *exact* date! All they would have to do is count seven years from the time all babies and Christians suddenly came up "missing."

If any questions remained, a trip to the cemetery would provide absolute proof that the rapture had occurred. By digging down into the graves of known Christians—a godly grandmother, a dedicated pastor, or a baby that had recently died—and finding their caskets empty, it would be evident the resurrection had taken place. It would not take long for thousands to know what had happened—and to figure the exact date for the end of the age. But since the scriptures teach that no man knows the day or hour when the end will come, it is evident that the rapture is not a separate event seven years before the end.

The description Jesus gave of his return rules out the idea of two separate events. "The Son of man shall come in the glory of his Father with his angels; and *then* he shall reward *every man* according to his works" (Matthew 16:27). This can not be a secret coming of Christ *alone*, for he comes in glory with the angels. It is at this time every man is rewarded. This can hardly fit the idea of the rapture being an earlier event, for in that case many would have already been caught up and rewarded!

"Whosoever therefore shall be ashamed of me and of my words in this adulterous and sinful generation, of him also shall the Son of man be ashamed, when he cometh in the glory of his Father with the holy angels" (Mark 8:38). If there had been an earlier coming of Christ, alone, in a secret rapture, whether he would be ashamed of people or not would have already taken place. Why, then, would he speak of these things in connection with his coming in glory with the angels?

14

The Christians at Thessalonica were enduring "persecutions and tribulations" and were being "troubled" by unbelievers (2 Thessalonians 1:4,7). But Paul encouraged them with the truth that they would be given "rest" from their troubles "when the Lord Jesus shall be revealed from heaven *with his mighty angels,* in flaming fire taking vengeance on them that know not God," for "he shall come to be glorified in his saints" (see 2 Thessalonians 1:7-10).

In this passage—as in the others—the reward of the righteous and the destruction that shall befall the wicked are interwoven with each other as to time, *both* occurring at the coming of the Lord. We notice also that when Jesus comes for the deliverance of his troubled saints, he comes in "flaming fire." No secret rapture here!

When will the Lord render vengeance to the wicked on one hand, and comfort to the saints on the other? The answer is clear: "WHEN the Lord Jesus shall be revealed from heaven with his mighty angels, in flaming fire, taking vengeance on them which know not God." The time of his being glorified in his saints is also the time when destruction will fall on the wicked. There is no interval of seven years between the two.

TWO STAGES OF ONE SECOND COMING?

The author's own study of the Bible, including Bible prophecy, began at an early age. While in my teens, I was stirred, like the people at Berea, to "search the scriptures daily" to see, for myself, what the Bible says (Acts 17:11). Most of the Christians I knew back then had been influenced by the "dispensational" interpretation of prophecy —that Jesus was coming back two more times: first in a secret rapture, then seven years later in glory and power at the end of the age. I knew Jesus had come the first time, and that "unto them that look for him shall he appear the *second* time without sin unto salvation" (Hebrews 9:28), but where did the scriptures teach a *third* coming of Christ? Most, of course, did not use the term third coming; it fit better to say there were "two stages" of the one second coming.

This wording seemed awkward to me—like something added to make a theory fit. If the rapture is a separate "stage" from the coming of Christ in power and glory, one wonders how each "stage" could be the *second* coming? If they are separate and distinct events—separated by several years—a coming that follows the second coming would be a third! But the scriptures never speak of a third coming, or of "comings" (plural), and the term "two second comings" is self-contradictory.

In an attempt to explain this difficulty, some dispensational writers go so far as to argue that the "rapture" is not the COMING of the Lord! One puts it this way: "Strictly speaking the rapture is NOT THE SECOND COMING AT ALL. The second coming is the visible, local, bodily appearing of Christ in the clouds of heaven as he returns to this earth...in power and great glory."[8] Another says: "The thrilling event which will both mark the end of the day of grace and open the door for the Great Tribulation is the rapture....Specifically speaking, THIS IS NOT THE SECOND COMING OF CHRIST. Rather this is the rapture, or the catching up, of the true church."[9]

But attempting to make the catching up a *separate* and *earlier* event from the coming of Christ, is glaringly inconsistent with the wording of scripture. Jesus said, "Be ye therefore also ready: for in such an hour as you think not the Son of man COMETH" (Matthew 24:44). Why would Jesus warn about being ready for the COMING of the Son of man, if the rapture takes place *before* his coming?

Jesus said: "Occupy till I COME" (Luke 19:13). How could the church occupy until he comes, if the church will be raptured away seven years before his coming? Jesus said: "I will COME again, and receive you unto myself" (John 14:3). Plainly it is when Jesus comes that he receives his people unto himself. The receiving is not seven years before his coming!

In perfect harmony with these teachings of Jesus, the apostles admonished: "Be patient then, brethren, unto the COMING of the Lord...for yet a little while, and he that shall COME will COME, and will not tarry" (James 5:7; Hebrews 10:36,37). Again, why exhort the brethren to be patient unto the COMING of the Lord, if their real hope was a rapture *before* his coming?

16

Paul speaks of Christians as "waiting for the COMING of our Lord Jesus Christ" (1 Corinthians 1:7). If he believed Christians would be caught up to heaven in a secret rapture seven years before the Lord's coming, why didn't he speak of Christians as waiting for that? Paul certainly did not consider the rapture a separate event. Even in the "rapture" passage, he comes right out and calls the catching up of believers "the COMING of the Lord"! (1 Thessalonians 4:15). In view of these things, we find it very strained for writers to make statements that the rapture is not the coming of the Lord.

DO GREEK WORDS DISTINGUISH TWO EVENTS?

But what about the meaning of the *Greek* words that are used to describe the second coming? One writer says: "The TWO phases of Christ's second coming are *clearly* distinguished in the Greek. The 'parousia'...is His coming for his saints....The 'apokalupsis' (the revealing, unveiling, making manifest) is his coming with his saints."[10] But, as we shall see, instead of the Greek words indicating two separate events, the various words are actually used *interchangeably!*

The following is a list of six Greek words that describe the second coming of Christ, the specific meaning of each, and a representative verse in which each word is used:

1. *Parousia* (the personal presence of one who comes and arrives): "Be patient...unto the *coming* of the Lord" (James 5:7).

2. *Apokalupsis* (appearing, revelation): "The Lord shall be *revealed* from heaven with his mighty angels" (2 Thessalonians 1:7).

3. *Epiphaneia* (manifestation, glory): "The *appearing* of our Lord Jesus Christ" (1 Timothy 6:14).

4. *Phaneroo* (to render apparent): "When he shall *appear*, we shall be like him" (1 John 3:2).

5. *Erchomai* (the act of coming, to come from one place to another): "Occupy till I *come*" (Luke 19:13).

6. *Heko* (the point of arrival): "Hold fast till I *come*" (Revelation 2:25).

The first word on our list, *parousia*, stresses the actual personal presence of one that has come and arrived. Noth-

17

ing in this word conveys the idea of *secrecy*. It was in common use, as when Paul spoke of the "coming *[parousia]* of Titus" (2 Corinthians 7:6), the "coming *[parousia]* of Stephanas" (1 Corinthians 16:17), and of his own "coming *[parousia]*" to Philippi (Philippians 1:26).

Paul used this word in the noted rapture passage which speaks of "the coming *[parousia]* of the Lord" when believers will be caught up to meet the Lord in the air (1 Thessalonians 4:15-17). But Paul's use of this word here can hardly mean a separate event from the Lord's coming at the end of the age, for in his second letter to the Thessalonians, he places the *parousia* AFTER the reign of the man of sin—not before! Speaking of "the coming *[parousia]* of our Lord" and "our gathering together unto him," Paul says "the Lord shall destroy [the man of sin] with the brightness of his coming *[parousia]*" (2 Thessalonians 2:8).

Peter, like Paul, spoke of the Lord's "coming *[parousia]*" at the end of the age, when "the heavens shall pass away with a great noise, and the elements shall melt with fervent heat." He exhorted Christians to be "looking for...the coming *[parousia]* of the day of God, wherein the heavens being on fire shall be dissolved, and the elements shall melt with fervent heat" (2 Peter 3:4-12). In none of these instances could *parousia* mean a pre-tribulation rapture.

It should also be noted here, the plural form of the word *parousia* is not used in connection with the Lord's coming. The definite article is consistently used. It is not *a* coming of the Lord, but *the* coming of the Lord.

Peter told Christians to "hope to the *end* for the grace that is to be brought unto you at the REVELATION *[apokalupsis]* of Jesus Christ" (1 Peter 1:13). Those who teach that Christ comes first in the RAPTURE, then seven years later in the REVELATION, face serious difficulties here. It would not be necessary for Christians to hope to the end for the grace to be brought to them at the REVELATION of Christ, if, in reality, this grace was to be given at a separate rapture seven years before! In the immediate context, Peter spoke of Christians being "found unto praise and honor and glory at the APPEARING *[apokalupsis—revelation]* of Jesus Christ" (verse 7). Christians are "waiting for the coming *[apokalupsis—revelation]* of our Lord Jesus Christ" (1 Corinthians 1:7). But, again, why would Christians be waiting for the "revelation" if the "rapture" comes seven years sooner?

According to the Bible, the *apokalupsis*—the revelation of Christ—is when Christians will be gathered; this is when they meet the Lord; this is the day for which they are waiting. The rapture, then, cannot be one event and the revelation a later event. Instead of two phases being "clearly distinguished in the Greek" by the terms *parousia* and *apokalupsis*, both are used in a way that points to one event, the second coming of Christ at the end of the age.

Another word used to describe the return of Christ, *epiphaneia*, speaks of manifestation and glory that will accompany our Lord when he comes. No one applies this to a secret, pre-tribulation coming, for Christ will slay the man of sin "with the brightness *[epiphaneia]* of his coming" (2 Thessalonians 2:8). Bearing this in mind, notice that Christians are to "...keep this commandment without spot, unrebukeable, until the appearing *[epiphaneia]* of our Lord Jesus Christ: which in his times he shall *show*...the King of kings and Lord of lords" (1 Timothy 6:14,15). Why would Christians be exhorted to keep the commandment until the *epiphaneia*—the glorious appearing—if the rapture was seven years before this?

The fourth word on our list, *phaneroo*, means to render apparent, referring to the open power and glory of Christ's coming. "When the chief Shepherd shall appear *[phaneroo]*, you shall receive a crown of glory" (1 Peter 5:4). If Christians had been raptured and crowned at an earlier coming of Christ, what sense would these words make? As John said: "We know that, when he shall appear *[phaneroo]*, we shall be like him; for we shall see him as he is" (1 John 3:2). As Christians it is when Christ shall come and appear—be rendered apparent—we shall be like him. Nothing here about an invisible coming!

Instead of the Greek terms indicating two separate events, just the opposite is the case. They are used interchangeably. Jesus said: "But as the days of Noah were, so shall also the COMING *[parousia]* of the son of man be" (Matthew 24:37). Luke's account of the *same* passage says: "As it was in the days of Noah...even thus shall it be in the day when the son of man is REVEALED [apokalupsis]" (Luke 17:26,30). "Therefore be ye also ready; for in such an hour as you think not the son of man COMETH [erchomai]" (Matthew 24:44). Here, then, parousia, apokalupsis, and erchomai are all used of the same event.

Erchomai, in turn, is used to describe the same event as heko: "For yet a little while, and he that shall COME [erchomai] will COME [heko], and will not tarry" (Hebrews 10:37). Heko and parousia are used together: "Where is the promise of his COMING [parousia]?....The day of the Lord will COME [heko] as a thief in the night" (2 Peter 3:10). Parousia and epiphaneia are linked together: the man of sin will be destroyed by the "BRIGHTNESS [epiphaneia]" of Christ's "COMING [parousia]" (2 Thessalonians 2:8). And, we know that the parousia is the phaneroo, for both expressions are used together: "And now, little children, abide in him; that, when he shall APPEAR [phaneroo], we may have confidence, and not be ashamed before him at his COMING [parousia]" (1 John 2:28).

Thus we see that all of these Greek words are used interchangeably. As in English, the different words present varied shades of meaning. But trying to split the second coming of Christ into two "stages" or "comings" on a supposed distinction in Greek terms is completely artificial.

When Jesus ascended into heaven and his disciples stood watching, two angels said: "You men of Galilee, why stand gazing up into heaven? this same Jesus, which is taken up from you into heaven, shall so come in like manner as you have seen him go into heaven" (Acts 1:11). The fact that they did not "see" him go into heaven in two ascensions, certainly argues against his second coming being in two stages.

COMING "FOR" AND "COMING" WITH THE SAINTS

What about the argument commonly given—that since the Lord will come "with" his saints (Jude 14), there must be an earlier coming of the Lord "for" the saints to take them to heaven? Actually, the Bible never uses the expression "coming FOR the saints." And the rapture text, instead of saying believers will be raptured to heaven, actually says they will be "caught up...in the clouds, to meet

20

the Lord in the *air*" (1 Thessalonians 4:16,17). Where they go, after meeting the Lord in the clouds, is not explained in this text.

When we are told that believers will rise to "MEET" the Lord in the air, the word is *apantesis*. It was used to describe the coming of a king or governor to visit a city, who, as he approached would be met by citizens who would then escort him on the last part of his journey into the city. If it has that same meaning here, as the Lord descends from heaven, believers will rise "to meet the Lord in the air," in order to *come* with him. This would not require a separate coming. *Apantesis* appears again in the parable of the ten virgins who "took their lamps, and went forth to MEET the bridegroom" (Matthew 25:1,6). After they went out to "meet" him, they returned "with him."

One final use of the word *apantesis* appears in connection with Paul's journey to Rome. "When the brethren heard of us, they came to MEET us as far as Appii forum...and when we came to Rome..." (Acts 28:14-16). Suppose the men who went to meet Paul told of their plans—that they heard Paul was coming to Rome and they were going to meet him. Whether they explained it or not, their going to meet him would imply they were coming back with him. None would understand this to mean they would meet Paul, go back to where he had been, spend some time there, in order to finally come *with* him to Rome!

The late Oswald J. Smith, noted missionary statesman, pastor, and song writer, sums it up in these words: "I learned, too, that the word for 'meet' in 1 Thessalonians 4...meant 'returning with' and not 'remaining at' the place of meeting. When the brethren from Rome met Paul, they immediately returned to the city with him. When the virgins met the bridegroom they accompanied him back to the wedding. When the saints meet Christ in the air...they will return *with* him....There is no secret rapture. That theory must be deliberately read into the passage."[11]

But regardless of how we take the word "meet" or the expression "coming with," Jude 14 can add no weight to the two-stage position. There are good reasons to believe the "saints" mentioned in this verse are the ANGELS who come with the Lord! "Behold, the Lord cometh with ten thousands of his saints," (Jude 14). The word translated "saints" is *hagios*, meaning simply "holy," or in this case, "holy [ones]." The word usage itself could indicate angels or men, but in this context we believe angels are meant.

The *Pulpit Commentary* says: "The 'ten thousands of his saints' is better rendered 'ten thousands of his holy ones'....For the 'holy ones' here intended are the *angels.*"[12] This fits perfectly with the words of Jesus who spoke of coming with the holy angels—holy being the same word, *hagios*, used in Jude 14. "The Son of man shall come in his glory, and all the holy *[hagios]* angels with him..." (Matthew 25:31). "Whosoever shall be ashamed of me...of him also shall the Son of man be ashamed, when he cometh...with the holy *[hagios]* angels" (Mark 8:38).

The expression "ten thousands of saints" (used in Jude 14) also appears in Deuteronomy 33:2, a passage generally regarded as referring to angels: "The Lord came from Sinai, and rose up from Seir unto them; he shined forth from mount Paran, and he came with ten thousands of saints." Again, the *Pulpit Commentary* points out that a better translation would be "ten thousands of holy ones," the reference being to angels.[13] The *Matthew Henry Commentary* makes the same point: "His appearance was glorious: he shone forth like the sun when he goes forth in his strength. Even Seir and Paran, two mountains at some distance, were illuminated by the divine glory which appeared on Mount Sinai....He came with his holy angels....Hence the law is said to be given by the disposition of angels, Acts 7:53; Hebrews 2:2."[14]

If the expression "ten thousands of saints" referred to angelic beings in Deuteronomy, it is not inconsistent to believe the *same* expression can mean angelic beings in Jude 14. This position finds further support in the context, for these holy ones are associated with Christ in executing judgment upon the ungodly. "Behold, the Lord cometh with ten thousands of his *hagios* [holy ones], to execute judgment upon...all that are ungodly" (Jude 14,15). We believe this will be the job of angelic beings, not that of Christians. As the scriptures say: "At the end of the world...the *angels* shall come forth, and sever the wicked

22

from among the just, and shall cast them into the furnace of fire" (Matthew 13:49,50). "The Lord Jesus shall be revealed from heaven with his mighty *angels*, in flaming fire taking vengeance on them that know not God" (2 Thessalonians 1:7).

IS IT SCRIPTURAL?

The author once read the entire New Testament through for the express purpose of listing all scriptures that teach the return of Christ will be in two stages. (All of the verses I found are listed on page 186 of this book.) My conclusion was the same as Oswald J. Smith: "We might go through all the writers of the New Testament, and we would fail to discover any indication of the so-called 'two-stages' of our Lord's coming....There is no verse in the Bible that even mentions it."[15]

This point is known and admitted by men of varied denominational backgrounds. Renowned Biblical expositor, G. Campbell Morgan, said: "The idea of a separate and secret coming of Christ is...without any Biblical basis whatsoever."[16] Or consider the following statement by Pat Robertson: "If we assume that the tribulation will be a future worldwide time of persecution, then I must say that Christians will indeed go through it. I do not find in the Bible the teaching that Christians will be 'raptured' prior to the tribulation....The Bible teaches two comings of Jesus—one his birth; the second, his coming again in triumph. There is no third coming for a secret rapture."[17]

Even men who believe in a pre-tribulation rapture have sometimes admitted there is no scripture for it. Wilfrid Meloon mentions how he once heard Charles Fuller say on his radio program, "There is not one verse in the entire New Testament which teaches a pre-tribulation rapture of the church—but, I still believe it."[18] He loved Charles Fuller, but was puzzled by this statement. How important, how major, can a doctrine be—whatever it is—if "not one verse" in the Bible teaches it?

Though the two-stage teaching is not actually mentioned in the Bible, Christians who believe this way feel it is justified by indirect evidence from certain "proof texts" we will now consider. First, Revelation 4:1: "After this I [John] looked, and, behold, a door was opened in heaven:

and the first voice which I heard was as it were of a trumpet talking with me; which said, Come up hither, and I will show thee things which must be hereafter."

A CLEAR PICTURE OF THE RAPTURE?

Scofield says: "This call seems *clearly* to indicate the fulfillment of 1 Thessalonians 4:14-17 [the rapture]. The word 'church' does not again occur in the Revelation till all is fulfilled."[19] De Haan, echoing this view, says: "This brief passage from Revelation is one of the shortest yet one of the *clearest* pictures in scripture of the rapture of the church."[20]

Since the word "church" does not appear in Revelation, chapters 4-18, the dispensational claim is that the church is absent from the earth during this time, and does not come into the picture again until chapter 19, which tells of the marriage supper and the coming of Christ as King of kings. But if the absence of the word "church" can prove the church is absent in chapters 4-18, we would have to conclude the church is also absent in chapter 19, for the word does not appear in that chapter either! Nor does it appear in chapter 20—or chapter 21! Only in a closing remark in the final chapter do we find these words: "I Jesus have sent mine angel to testify unto you these things in the *churches*"—not the universal church as a whole, but the seven churches of Asia (Revelation 22:16).

While the word "church" does not appear after chapter three until the last part of Revelation, the church is *not* absent in those chapters. In Revelation 13:7, we read that the beast would "make war with the saints." Verse 10 mentions the "patience and faith of the saints"—patience and faith in the midst of persecution! The "saints" are again mentioned in chapter 16, verse 6. In chapter 17 we read about the Babylonian woman "drunken with the blood of the saints" (verse 6) and that "in her was found the blood of the saints" (Revelation 18:24).

The dispensational position is that the saints mentioned in these chapters are not church saints, but tribulation saints. Yet when we find the word "saints" in chapter 19, we are told this refers to the church! "The marriage of the Lamb is come, and his wife hath made herself ready.

And to her was granted that she should be arrayed in fine linen, clean and white: for the fine linen is the righteousness of saints" (Revelation 19:7,8). The Scofield footnote says: "The 'Lamb's wife' here is the 'bride,' the *Church.* "[21] But to be consistent, if the saints in Revelation 19 are church saints, how can some rightly argue that the saints mentioned in the chapter before (chapter 18), the chapter before that (chapter 17), the chapter before that (chapter 16), and chapter 13 are some different kind of saints? This is arbitrary.

The rapture is not the subject of Revelation 4:1, it simply records the experience of John—in spirit—being taken into the heavenly realm. This does not prove we should look for the church in heaven any more than his being taken into the wilderness, to Babylon, would prove the church was there! (Revelation 17:3-5). As the various scenes of Revelation unfold, John is represented as being different places—on the earth (he sees an angel "come down [not go down] from heaven"—Revelation 10:1, 18:1), he measures what is, apparently, an earthly temple, for its courts are trodden down by Gentiles (Revelation 11:1), he stands upon the sand of the sea and watches a beast rise from its waters (Revelation 13:1). Plainly, John cannot be a *consistent* type of the church in heaven during these chapters.

KEPT FROM THE "HOUR OF TEMPTATION"

Another dispensational "proof text," also from the book of Revelation, contains the words of Jesus to the church at Philadelphia: "Because thou hast kept the word of my patience, I also will keep thee from the hour of temptation, which shall come upon all the world, to try them that dwell upon the earth" (Revelation 3:10). Those who use this verse in defense of the secret rapture position must assume the "hour of temptation" is the same as what they call "The Great Tribulation Period" at the end of this age. They must then assume that being kept from this temptation requires being raptured out of this world!

In its primary application, this promise would have pertained to the church of Philadelphia, located in Asia Minor, in the first century. Were the people of this church kept from a world-wide time of temptation? As sure as the promise is true, they were. But this did not require a rapture. We believe they were kept by the power and grace of God. If God fulfilled his promise to them, the "hour of temptation"—whatever might be the precise meaning of this expression—would have occurred in their day. This could hardly offer proof for a secret rapture to escape a great tribulation period 2,000 years later.

Some believe the seven churches of Asia represent seven successive ages of the church, extending from the first century to the rapture. If so, then the message to the church at Philadelphia could not refer to the rapture, for Philadelphia would be the sixth church in the succession, not the last (the seventh)! If the message to the Philadelphia church proves an escape rapture, the church ages would have to be 1,2,3,4,5,7,6!

We believe Christians can be kept from an hour of temptation—in any age—without being raptured out of the world! This principle can be established by comparing the following scriptures:

> Because thou hast *kept* the *word* of my patience, I also will *keep* thee from the hour of *temptation,* which shall come upon all the world, to try them that dwell upon the earth. (Revelation 3:10).

> They have *kept* thy *word.*...I pray not that thou shouldest take them out of the world, but that thou shouldest *keep* them from the *evil.* (John 17:6,15).

Both of these passages are the words of Jesus. Both were recorded by John. The people in both passages have kept the word. Because they have kept the word, God will "keep them." In one passage they are kept from the hour of *temptation;* in the other, they are kept from *evil.* These are closely related terms, as in the Lord's prayer: "Lead us not into temptation, but deliver us from evil" (Matthew 6:13). If believers can be kept from the evil of the world without being taken out of the world—as in the one passage—it is certain they don't have to be raptured away from temptation in the other.

Though Revelation 3:10 probably had a specific meaning and fulfillment to the Philadelphia church of the first century, here also is a promise of God's keeping power in any hour of temptation, in any century, any year, any day—not just the last seven years of this age. Paul wrote: "There hath no temptation taken you but such as is common to man, but God...will not suffer you to be *tempted* above that you are able; but will with the temptation also make a way of *escape* that you may be able to bear it" (1 Corinthians 10:12,13). "The Lord knoweth how to deliver the godly out of temptations" (2 Peter 2:9). Jabez prayed: "*Keep* me from evil...and God granted him that which he requested" (1 Chronicles 4:10). And we, today, can also be "*kept* by the power of God through faith unto salvation" (1 Peter 1:5), for God "is able to *keep* you from falling" (Jude 24). God's keeping power and escape from temptation can be provided without a secret rapture!

"ESCAPE"—FROM WHAT?

One more text should be noticed here: "Watch therefore and *pray* always, that you may be accounted worthy to ESCAPE all these things that shall come to pass, and to stand before the Son of man" (Luke 21:36). Here is a verse about praying for "escape," but again, nothing about the church being raptured out of this world in order for this to be accomplished! In the prayer of Jesus, he said: "I pray NOT that thou shouldest take them out of the world, but that thou shouldest keep them from the evil" (John 17:15). Would Jesus pray one way and tell the disciples to pray another way?

With what is this word "escape" connected? Is it escape from a *period of time*—a dispensational great tribulation during the last seven years of this age? It does not say so. A look at the context shows the reference is to "THAT DAY," the time believers will be gathered to meet the Lord in the air and destruction shall fall upon the world. "Heaven and earth shall pass away [the end of the age]...take heed to yourselves, lest at any time your hearts be overcharged with surfeiting, and drunkenness, and cares of this life, and so THAT DAY come upon you unawares. For as a snare shall it come on all them that dwell on the face of the whole earth. Watch therefore, and pray always, that you may be accounted worthy to escape all these things that shall come to pass, and to stand before the Son of man" (Luke 21:33-36). If believers were to no longer be on the earth—if they were to be raptured away

27

seven years before the end—how could "that day" possibly come upon them unawares?

Jesus promised that those who are prayerfully watching and not overcharged with eating and drinking will escape the destruction of THAT DAY. The same basic message was presented by Paul: "THE DAY of the Lord so cometh as a thief in the night. For when they shall say, Peace and safety; then *sudden destruction* cometh upon them as travail upon a woman with child; and they shall *not escape*. But you, brethren, are not in darkness that THAT DAY should overtake you as a thief. You are all the children of the light...we are not of the night....Therefore let us not sleep, as do others; but let us *watch*...for God hath not appointed us to wrath, but to obtain salvation by our Lord Jesus Christ" (1 Thessalonians 5:1-9).

Notice how this passage also mentions THAT DAY. It will bring "sudden destruction" upon unbelievers "and they shall *not* escape." Christians, however, will escape. They are not appointed to wrath. They will be caught up to meet the Lord in the clouds while destruction falls on the earth below.

WILL CHRIST RETURN "AT ANY MOMENT"?

Did the early Christians believe the rapture could occur at *any* moment? Or did they believe there were certain things that would be fulfilled *first?*

We believe there is conclusive proof in the New Testament that the early church did *not* hold the any moment teaching. Jesus pointed out that no man knows the time of his return and that we should live a life of watchfulness and obedience at all times. However, Jesus himself taught certain things would happen first.

When Jesus told his disciples of the second coming, he was still with them *in person.* Obviously the ascension had to precede the return. And before his ascension, of course, was to be Calvary: "First must he suffer many things, and be rejected of this generation" (Luke 17:25).

Jesus told his disciples that after his ascension, he would send the Holy Spirit upon them. This would take place, obviously, *before* Christ would come again. Thus, prior to Pentecost, we see the disciples waiting—not for the second coming of Christ—but the coming of the Holy Spirit to endue them with power. Being filled with the Holy Spirit they were to go into all the world and teach all nations (Acts 1:8). Time had to be allowed for travel, preaching, baptizing, instructing converts, etc. Surely Jesus would not return before they had time to do what he had commissioned them to do!

Jesus predicted the destruction of Jerusalem and told his disciples: "When you see Jerusalem compassed with armies, then know that the desolation thereof is nigh. Then let them which are in Judea flee to the mountains" (Luke 21:21). At the second coming of Christ, there will be no need for Christians to flee into the mountains, for they will be caught up to meet the Lord in the air! The destruction of Jerusalem, then, was to be an event *before* the second coming of Christ. Living on this side of the fulfillment, we know Jerusalem was destroyed in 70 A.D.

Jesus also explained that Peter would grow old and die—BEFORE the second coming! When thou shalt be old," Jesus said to Peter, "thou shalt stretch forth thy hands, and another shall gird thee, and carry thee whither thou wouldest not. This spake he, signifying by what death he would glorify God" (John 21:18,19; cf. 2 Peter 1:14). Then Peter asked if John would live to see the coming of the Lord. Jesus replied: "If I will that he tarry till I come, what is that to thee? follow thou me." On the basis of this statement, a saying spread "among the brethren, that that disciple [John] should not die: yet Jesus said not unto him, he shall not die; but, If I will that he tarry till I come, what is that to thee?" (John 21:20-23). Whether John would live to see the second coming was not answered, but in the case of Peter, it was definitely stated he would grow old and die before the Lord's return.

We believe the early Christians lived in an expectation and hope of the second coming; for, whether alive at that time, or because of the resurrection, they would all ultimately share in the glory of that day! But they did not believe his coming would be at any moment; they knew certain things would happen first.

Writing to the Thessalonians, Paul spoke of the resurrection and catching up of believers to meet the Lord in the air (1 Thessalonians 4:16,17). Later, some confusion developed in their minds about this glorious event, and in his second epistle, Paul clarified the matter. His remarks show he did not hold the any-moment position:

> Now we beseech you, brethren, by [concerning] the coming of our Lord Jesus Christ, and by [concerning] our *gathering together* unto him, that you be not soon shaken in mind, or be troubled, neither by spirit, nor by word, nor by letter as from us, as that the day of Christ is at hand. Let no man deceive you by any means: for that day shall *not* come, except there come a falling away *first*, and that man of sin be revealed, the son of perdition. (2 Thessalonians 2:1-3).

Here, then, two things are mentioned that Christians would witness *before* the day of Christ's coming to gather believers unto himself. There would be a falling away and the man of sin would be revealed. Concerning these very things, the inspired apostle said: "Let no man deceive you"! Let us beware, then, of a teaching which says the church will be raptured to heaven BEFORE the man of sin is revealed. According to Paul, the order of events would be: (1) a falling away, (2) the man of sin would be revealed, and (3) the coming of Christ and our gathering together unto him. It is plain. But according to the any moment view, instead of these events being in this order, they would have to be: 3, then 1, and then 2! That is: (3) the coming of Christ and our gathering together unto him, (1) a falling away, and (2) the man of sin revealed: 3,1,2, or perhaps 3,2,1, instead of 1,2,3!

In an attempt to justify this reversal of events, some teach that the falling away is a departure—the departure of the church in the rapture! But the word translated "falling away" is *apostasia*, meaning apostasy, a departure from the truth, a well established meaning. To attempt to make "falling away" mean "catching up" shows how hard pressed the dispensational arrangement is!

Paul said believers would witness certain events first: the falling away, the man of sin would be revealed, and then the gathering together to meet the Lord at his coming. But if the falling away meant the rapture—an exodus of believers from the world—they would not witness the events that followed, for they would not be here! Paul's words would have no bearing on the point he was making.

Being "troubled" with "persecutions and tribulations," the believers at Thessalonica wondered if the day of Christ was not right "at hand" (2 Thessalonians 1,2). If Paul had believed in the any moment position, here was his perfect opportunity to encourage them with the teaching that Jesus was coming *soon*—at any moment. He might have written something like this: "Now we beseech you, brethren, concerning the coming of our Lord Jesus Christ and our gathering together unto him, that you be not soon shaken in mind, for *nothing needs to happen first*. That day shall come *before* the falling away and *before* the man of sin is revealed. Yes, our gathering together unto him could happen *at any moment!*"

But to the contrary, this was *not* his answer. Instead, he explained there would be a falling away, and the man of sin would be revealed, before the day of Christ! There can be no mistake that "the day of Christ" refers to the rapture, for it is used in reference to "our gathering together unto him" (2 Thessalonians 2). Christians are "waiting" for the "day of the Lord Jesus Christ" (1 Corinthians 1:7-9). It is "in the day of the Lord Jesus" that they will be gathered and "rejoice" at seeing each other (2 Corinthians 1:14). The "good work" begun in Christians must continue "until the day of the Lord Jesus Christ" (Philippians 1:6). Paul admonished the Philippian believers to be "sincere and without offence" until "the day of Christ" (verse 10), when he would see them and rejoice that his labor had not been in vain (Philippians 2:16). All of these verses plainly show that the "day of Christ" is the time when believers are gathered to meet Christ.

Scofield, attempting to deal with the glaring problem dispensationalism faces here, says that the King James Version "has 'day of Christ,' 2 Thessalonians 2:2, incorrectly, for 'day of the Lord'."[22] Apparently some ancient manuscripts have it one way and some another. But what difference does this make? We use the expression "the coming of the *Lord*" when referring to "the coming of *Christ.*" Why try to make the New Testament expression "the day of the *Lord*" mean something different than "the day of *Christ"?* Only to defend a hard pressed theory would any make this distinction. The following terms are all used *interchangeably* in reference to the Lord's coming to gather believers:

"The day of Christ" (Philippians 1:10).

"The day of Jesus Christ" (Philippians 1:6).

"The day of our Lord Jesus Christ" (1 Corinthians 1:8).

"The day of the Lord Jesus" (2 Corinthians 1:14).

"The day of the Lord" (1 Thessalonians 5:2).

We think it is inconsistent to try to make the last expression mean a different "Lord" or a different time than the other terms describe. The day of the Lord *is* the day of Christ in New Testament usage. And according to Paul, that day—when believers will be gathered unto him—will not come until AFTER the man of sin has been revealed!

WHEN DID IT BEGIN?

The teaching that there will be a secret coming of Christ *before* the appearance of the man of sin has been widely taught—and believed—in this century. Many fine Christians have accepted it with little or no investigation. But, as shocking as it may sound, this teaching was not the position of the early church, was not taught by the reformers, WAS NOT TAUGHT BY ANYONE UNTIL AROUND THE YEAR 1830! If this is true, then the secret, pre-tribulation rapture teaching is not a part of the true original faith that was once delivered unto the saints! It is not the old time gospel.

George Ladd, seminary professor, after making a survey of church history says: *"Every* church father who deals with this subject expects the *church* to suffer at the hands of Antichrist...we can find no trace of pretribulationism in the early church: and no modern pretribulationist has successfully proved that this particular doctrine was held by any of the church fathers or students of the word before the nineteenth century."[23]

This is quite a sweeping statement, but one which we believe will stand up under investigation. *The Didache*, one of the earliest pieces of Christian literature written after the New Testament, stated that the Antichrist would come, that many would be offended and lost, and the resurrection of the just would follow this time of woe.[24] The *Epistle of Barnabas*, written about the same time, says: "When the Son comes, he will destroy the time of the Wicked one and will judge the godless"—thus placing the coming of Christ after the reign of the Wicked one, not before. He did not hold to an any moment return of Christ, for he expected the Roman empire to fall first.[25]

Justin Martyr (100-165) spoke of the coming of the Lord in these words: "He shall come from heaven with glory, when the man of apostasy, who speaks strange things against the most High, shall venture to do unlawful deeds on earth *against us Christians*, who, have learned the true worship of God from the law, and the word which went forth from Jerusalem by means of the apostles of Jesus." Christ "shall come from heaven with glory, accompanied by his angelic hosts, when also he shall raise the bodies of all men who have lived, and shall clothe those of the worthy with immortality."[26]

Irenaeus (130-202) spoke of "the resurrection of the just, which takes place *after* the coming of Antichrist ....But when this Antichrist shall have devastated all things in this world...*then* the Lord shall come from heaven in the clouds, in the glory of the Father, sending this man and those who follow him into the lake of fire; but bringing in for the righteous the times of the kingdom." He spoke of kings who "shall give their kingdom to the beast, and put the *church* to flight. After that they shall be destroyed by the coming of our Lord....In the *end* the church shall be suddenly caught up" and, having overcome, will be "crowned with incorruption."[27]

Tertullian (160-240) believed that Antichrist would rise to power and persecute the *church*. He affirmed it was customary for Christians to pray for a part in the resurrection to meet Christ at the *end* of the world.[28]

Hippolytus (170-236) spoke of the four empires of Daniel and that the breaking up of the fourth empire (which was then in power) would bring on the dreaded Antichrist who would persecute the *church*. He believed the second advent would be the time that the dead would be raised, Antichrist destroyed, and the saints glorified.[29]

Cyprian (200-258), a Christian bishop and martyr, believed Antichrist would reign, *after* which Christ would come at the *end* of the world.[30]

Lactantius (260-330) believed the Antichrist would reign over the world and afflict *the righteous*, but that God would send a Great King to rescue them, to destroy the wicked with fire and sword, to raise the dead and renew the world.[31]

Cyril (315-386), bishop of Jerusalem, wrote: "We believe in Him, who also ascended into the heavens, and sat down on the right hand of the Father, and shall come in glory to judge the quick and dead...at the *end* of this world, in *the last day*. For of this world there is to be an end, and this created world is to be re-made anew." It is evident, from various statements, that he believed Antichrist would come to power and persecute the church before the second coming of Christ.[32]

The essence of the teaching of these early writers is that Antichrist would persecute the church, that the coming of Christ would follow and bring an end to the reign of Antichrist, that the end of the world would be the time of resurrection when believers will be gathered to meet the Lord.

Those who hold the pre-tribulation position have sometimes quoted Irenaeus: "And therefore, when in the end the church shall be suddenly caught up it is said, 'There shall be tribulation such as has not been since the beginning neither shall be.' For this is the last contest of the righteous, in which, when they overcome, they are crowned with incorruption."[33] While it is true a part of this passage might seem to teach a pre-tribulation rapture, reading the whole passage shows this was not the intended meaning.

He spoke of tribulation as the "last" contest of the righteous and in overcoming they would be crowned. He spoke of the "end" as the time when the church will be suddenly caught up. We saw earlier that Irenaeus believed Antichrist would persecute the church and that after this Christ would come to reward the righteous and destroy the wicked. Certainly this was not the pre-tribulation position of dispensationalism.

A collection of visions, exhortations, and parables circulated around 150 A.D., known as the *Shepherd of Hermas*, has been cited. In one place the writer tells of meeting, and escaping from, what appeared to be a huge beast. A short distance on down the road, a virgin dressed in white told him that even as he escaped from the beast, those who truly repent would escape the great tribulation: "If then you prepare yourselves, and repent with all your heart and turn to the Lord, it will be possible for you to escape it, if your heart be pure and spotless."[34]

Though this passage speaks about escape from the great tribulation, we should not read into it things that are not there. Nothing is said about a secret rapture to take the church out of this world, nothing about two second comings of Christ or the accompanying dispensational teachings. Other passages of the *Shepherd of Hermas* present the view (commonly held by the early Christians) that tribulations and persecutions have a purifying effect on the church. Vision Two, for example, says: "Happy are ye who *endure* the great tribulation that is coming on, and happy are they who shall not deny their own life."[35] It would be quite difficult to build a pre-tribulation doctrine on this somewhat obscure book.

Looking on down through the centuries, there are certain names that stand out in Christian history: John Wyclif, John Huss, Martin Luther, Philipp Melanchthon, Huldreich Zwingli, William Tyndale, Nicholas Ridley, Hugh Latimer, John Foxe, Edwin Sandys, John Calvin, John Knox, King James, Isaac Newton, Thomas Newton, John Wesley. NONE of these men believed the church would be taken out before the appearance of Antichrist. They believed the church would suffer at the hands of Antichrist whose career would be ended by the return of Christ.

But today, many Christians have been taught the rapture will take them to heaven, before the Antichrist, and before Christ comes in power and glory. This teaching is of comparatively modern origin, dating from around 1830, and developing in the years that followed. Names associated with what was then a new teaching include Irving, McDonald, and Darby. First, we will notice the name of Edward Irving.

Born in Scotland in 1792, Irving was one of the most eloquent preachers of his time. In 1828 his open air meetings in Scotland drew crowds of 10,000 people. His church in London seated one thousand people and was packed week after week. When he wrote a tract  inferring Jesus possessed a fallen human nature, however, a controversy arose among his people and he was removed from his pulpit in 1832, though the larger part of his congregation stood by him and sought for a new meeting place. An ecclesiastical trial in 1833 deprived him of his status as a clergyman in the Church of Scotland. His death the following year, 1834, at Glasgow, was attributed to tuberculosis and a broken heart.[36]

In September, 1830, Irving's journal, "The Morning Watch," carried an article which featured a two stage idea concerning the return of Christ. Some feel the seeds of this doctrine may have been a Spanish book, *The Coming of the Messiah in Glory and Majesty*, written by Manuel Lacunza, which Irving translated into English in 1827.[37] This book, originally published in 1812, said that "when the Lord returns from heaven to earth, upon his coming forth from heaven, and *much before* his arrival at the earth, he will give his orders, and send forth his commandment...with a shout...with the voice of the archangel, and with the trump of God. At this voice of the Son of God, those who hear it, shall forthwith arise."[38]

It is not clear just what he meant by "much before." Some believe he may have meant a few hours, which would be "much before" compared to the five or six minutes some were teaching. In any event, Lacunza linked the catching up of believers to passages such as Revelation 19, Matthew 24:30, and Revelation 1:7. This was still a long way from the now-popular dispensational teaching.

Though Lacunza was a Roman Catholic, Pope Leo XII placed his book on the list of prohibited books—and no wonder: Lacunza taught that the Roman Catholic priesthood would eventually become the two-horned beast of Revelation 13!

An acquaintance of Irving, Miss Margaret McDonald, is another name commonly associated with the early beginnings of the two stage idea. In a prophetic utterance given in the spring of 1830, she spoke of a coming of Christ that would be seen only by those whose eyes were spiritually open. She wrote an account of this and sent handwritten copies to various Christian leaders of the time. A book published by Robert Norton in 1840, *The Restoration of Apostles and Prophets In the Catholic Apostolic Church*, now very rare, gave a printed account of her revelation.[39] From this account, we will now quote the pertinent portions of this utterance:

> Now there is distress of nations, with perplexity, the seas and the waves roaring, men's hearts failing them for fear—now look out for the sign of the Son of man. Here I was made to stop and cry out, O it is not known what the sign of the Son of man is...I felt this needed to be revealed, and that there was great darkness and error about it; but suddenly what it was burst upon me with a glorious light. I saw it was just the Lord himself descending from Heaven with a shout, just the glorified man, even Jesus...I saw the error to be, that men think that it will be something seen by the natural eye; but 'tis spiritual discernment that is needed....Only those who have the light of God within them will see the sign of his appearance....'tis only those that are alive in him that will be caught up to meet him in the air....I repeated frequently, but the spiritual temple must and shall be reared, and the fullness of Christ be poured into his body, and then shall we be caught up to meet him.

The church over the centuries had believed in the open, visible, glorious coming of the Lord. But in the McDonald utterance, something *not known* before was presented—a coming of the Lord *alone*, a coming *not seen* by the natural eye, a coming to catch up those who would be spiritually alive. Here then are hints of an earlier coming—before the open and visible coming of the Lord—but her exact position is not always clearly defined.

Unlike the escape rapture theory in its present form, Miss McDonald went on to speak of great testing to befall the church.

> The Wicked will be revealed, with all power and signs and lying wonders, so that if it were possible the very elect will be deceived.—This is the fiery trial which is to try *us*.—It will be for the purging and purifying of the real members of the body of Jesus; but Oh it will be a fiery trial...I frequently said that night, and often since, now shall the awful sight of a false Christ be seen on this earth, and nothing but the living Christ in *us* can detect this awful attempt of the enemy to deceive....This is particularly the nature of the trial, through which those are to pass who will be counted worthy to stand before the Son of man....The trial of the *Church* is from *Antichrist*....Oh be filled with the Spirit....This is what we are at present made to pray much for, that speedily we may all be made ready to meet our Lord in the air—and it will be.

The Protestant churches at the time, and for centuries, held to historicism: that the Papacy was the man of sin or Antichrist who was making war against the saints, that the church was already in tribulations, that purifying trials were the lot of the church. They believed the book of Revelation described events that spanned the centuries until the return of Christ. The famous Albury conferences taught that the church had now lived through the events of Revelation as far as chapter 16. (The idea that they were nearing a rapture at Revelation 4:1 was unknown!) Reading the entire wording of Margaret McDonald's utterance indicates her thinking was still that of the old historicist school of prophetic thought—but with a unique addition: the idea of a secret coming.

Soon the secret coming teaching was being taught among the group known as the Plymouth Brethren—to be accepted by some and rejected by others. In 1864, S.P. Tregelles, one of the Brethren that rejected this *new* teaching, wrote: "I am not aware that there was any definite teaching that there should be a secret rapture of the church at a secret coming until this was given forth as an 'utterance' in Mr. Irving's church from what was then received as being the voice of the Spirit. But whether any one ever asserted such a thing or not it was from that sup-

38

posed revelation that the modern doctrine and the modern phraseology respecting it arose. It came, not from the Holy Scripture, but from that which falsely pretended to be the Spirit of God."[40]

Strangely enough, what at first was understood to be a new and special revelation—the teaching there would be a separate coming to rapture those that were ready—was soon to be dogmatically promoted AS THOUGH IT HAD ALWAYS BEEN THE ETERNAL TRUTH OF THE SCRIPTURES!

In the years that follow-ed, the two stage teaching was developed further by John Nelson Darby (1800-1882). Irving apparently taught some kind of secret rapture, and there was the utterance of Margaret McDonald that made the rounds, but it was Darby who introduced it into the main current of prophetic interpretation.

Darby was a brilliant and well educated man whose writings on Biblical subjects number over 30 volumes of 600 pages each. He produced a translation of the Bible with notes, also wrote poems and hymns. In 1825, he was ordained a deacon in the Church of England. He later became a leader among the Plymouth Brethren, a movement which was composed largely of people who had become dissatisfied with the lethargic condition that prevailed in many of the churches. Though the movement had its beginning in Dublin, it was Plymouth, England, that became the center of their literature outreach, thus the name Plymouth Brethren.

Darby's biographers refer to him as "the father of modern dispensationalism." Many of the Plymouth Brethren accepted his dispensational teachings and were sometimes called Darbyites. But not all of the Plymouth Brethren accepted his position. B.W. Newton rejected the two-stage view as "nonsense." Other noted ministers of the time —among them George Muller, William Booth, and Charles Spurgeon—also opposed this theory as being unscriptural.

The secret rapture was introduced into the United States and Canada in the 1860s and 1870s, though there is some indication it may have been taught as early as the 1840s. Darby himself visited the United States six times. The "new" teaching was spreading.

Following the lead of Darby, the writings of Charles Henry Mackintosh (1820-1896), commonly known as C.H.M., helped spread the dispensational theory. William Blackstone wrote a book, *Jesus is Coming*, which taught the secret rapture position. It was distributed to ministers and people of various denominations throughout the country. But probably the biggest single factor that contributed to the spread of the pre-tribulation teaching was the printing of the *Scofield Reference Bible* in 1909.

SCOFIELD AND DISPENSATIONALISM

Cyrus Ingerson Scofield (1843-1921) was a soldier during the Civil War. Later he took up law and politics. During the administration of President Grant, he was appointed U.S. Attorney to Kansas. In 1879, at St. Louis, he received Christ as savior. Three years later he became a Congregational minister. His first pastorate was at Dallas, Texas, where Dallas Theological Seminary still promotes the dispensational views he made popular through the notes of the *Scofield Reference Bible*. Whether he first heard about dispensationalism from Malachi Taylor, a member of the Plymouth Brethren, or J. H. Brooks, is not certain. He was definitely influenced by Darby, whom he considered "the most profound Bible student of modern times."[41]

Some have written about Scofield's divorce (from a Roman Catholic woman) and remarriage. Some believe the "Dr." in front of his name was self-given. Others have questioned some of his financial dealings and membership in a prestigious club. We will leave a discussion of those things, now long past, to others. In many ways Scofield stood for sound principles of evangelical Christianity. But his dispensationalism, being of comparatively modern origin, should be rejected.

Because of the Scofield Bible, many were led to believe in a secret rapture. Oswald J. Smith was one of them. But later he would write: "Now, after years of study and prayer, I am absolutely convinced that there will be no rapture *before* the tribulation...I believed the other theory simply because I was taught it by W.E. Blackstone in his book *Jesus is Coming,* the *Scofield Reference Bible* and prophetic conferences and Bible schools; but when I began to search the scriptures for myself I discovered that there is not a single verse in the Bible that upholds the pretribulation theory."[42]

Philip Mauro (1859-1952), one of the great Biblical scholars of the past century, had a similar experience. "It is mortifying to remember," he wrote, "that I not only held and taught these novelties myself, but that I even enjoyed a complacent sense of superiority because thereof, and regarded with feelings of pity and contempt those who had not received the ÷new light' and were unacquainted with this up-to-date method of ÷rightly dividing the word of truth'....The time came...when the inconsistencies and self-contradictions of the system itself, and above all, the impossibility of reconciling its main positions with the plain statements of the Word of God, became so glaringly evident that I could not do otherwise than to renounce it."[43]

G. Campbell Morgan (1863-1945), when asked if he believed in the two-stage view, said this about his experience: "Emphatically not! I know this view very well. In the earlier years of my ministry I taught it and incorporated it in my book *(God's Method With Man).* But further study so convinced me of the error of this teaching that I actually went to the expense of buying the plates from the publishers and destroying them. The idea of a separate and secret coming of Christ is a vagary of prophetic interpretation without any Biblical basis whatsoever."[44]

In all due respect to those who still hold the secret rapture teaching—some dear friends and fellow ministers being among that number—it is our sincere conviction that it should be rejected, first, because it lacks solid scriptural support, and, secondly, because of its comparatively recent origin. Though the secret rapture position still receives a lot of publicity, there are many within the body of Christ who are taking a second look at the rapture question. There is a distinct turning back to the original, apostolic, historical position.

* * * * * * * * * *

In part one of this book, we have considered the question of whether the rapture will be *before* or *after* the tribulation. In the section that follows, we will go a step further and look at the tribulation itself. What does the Bible teach about the great tribulation? Will it take place during the last seven years of this age? These questions bring us to a study of Matthew 24.

Part Two:

THE GREAT TRIBULATION
—Future or Fulfilled?

Studies in Matthew Twenty-four

It was a shocking statement Jesus made to his disciples. As they left the temple in Jerusalem, certain ones remarked about what a magnificent temple it was and how splendid were its *stones*. But Jesus said the time would come when one stone would not be left upon another that would not be thrown down! This statement aroused questions from the disciples. As they sat upon the mount of Olives, they asked Jesus *when* these things would happen and *what sign* would be given when these things were about to be fulfilled. In answer to these questions, Jesus spoke about deceivers, wars, earthquakes, famines, pestilences, the "abomination of desolation," and great tribulation.

Christians who hold the FUTURIST interpretation apply the verses about deceivers, wars, earthquakes, famines, and pestilences to our time—as things leading up to the tribulation period which they believe will be the last seven years of this age (after the rapture). The abomination of desolation is regarded as an idol of the Antichrist (or the Antichrist himself) to be set up in the holy of holies of a rebuilt Jewish temple at Jerusalem. When this happens, according to this position, the Jews will flee into the mountains, for then shall be great tribulation.

The FULFILLED interpretation, on the other hand, holds that the deceivers, wars, earthquakes, famines, and pestilences were things which Jesus said would *soon* happen—things that happened before the destruction of the temple. The abomination of desolation, by comparing the parallel accounts, was Gentile *armies* that surrounded Jerusalem to cause its desolation. Upon heeding the warning of Jesus, the disciples fled from Jerusalem and Judea. What Jesus called "great tribulation" referred to the judgment that fell upon the Jewish nation, resulting in the destruction of Jerusalem and the temple in 70 A.D.

Obviously the two interpretations—the FUTURIST and the FULFILLED—are far apart. Doubtless, there are fine Christians on both sides. But we feel many have accepted the futurist view, only because they have not been fully aware of the historical fulfillment. The prophecy is recorded in Matthew 24, Mark 13, and Luke 21. In order to get the *full* picture, the careful student will read all three accounts. Sometimes a detail not fully explained in one, is explained in the other.

The statement Jesus made about the temple being destroyed is recorded in all three accounts (Matthew 24:1,2; Mark 13:1,2; Luke 21:5,6):

Verily I say unto you, *there shall not be left here one stone upon another, that shall not be thrown down.*

"WHEN shall *these things* be?" the disciples asked, "and what shall be the *sign* when all *these things* shall be fulfilled?" In addition to the questions about the destruction of the temple, Matthew (but only Matthew) recorded the question: "What shall be the sign of thy coming, and of the end of the world?" We believe Jesus answered all of these questions. Nevertheless, the *primary* questioning —recorded by all the writers—was about the destruction of the temple: "When shall these things be?"

DECEIVERS

First, Jesus warned about deceivers (Matthew 24:4,5; Mark 13:5,6; Luke 21:8):

Take heed that no man deceive you. For *many* shall come in my name saying, I am Christ, and shall deceive *many.*

All three accounts warn about deceivers, but Luke's account explains *when* these things would happen: "And the time DRAWETH NEAR: go not therefore after them." This was not something that would take place hundreds or thousands of years later! Jesus was warning his disciples about something that was about to happen *in their time!*

Did "many" deceivers deceive "many" people in those days? Yes! According to the historian Josephus, twelve years after our Savior's death, a certain impostor named Theudas persuaded a multitude to follow him to the river Jordan which he claimed would divide for their passage. At the time of Felix (who is mentioned in the book of Acts), the country of the Jews was filled with impostors who Felix had put to death *every day*—a statement which indicates there were many of them! An Egyptian who "pretended to be a prophet" gathered 30,000 men, claiming he would show "how, at his command, the walls of Jerusalem would fall down."

Another deceiver was Simon, the sorcerer, who led people to believe he was the great power of God (see Acts 8). According to Irenaeus, he claimed to be the Son of God and creator of angels. Justin tells how he went to Rome and was acclaimed as a god by his magical powers.

Origen mentions a certain wonder-worker, Dositheus, who claimed he was the Christ foretold by Moses. Another deceiver in those days was Barchochebas who claimed to vomit flames. Bar-jesus, mentioned in Acts 13:6, was a sorcerer and false prophet. These are examples of the deceivers of whom history says there were "a great number," and of whom Jesus had prophesied there would be "many."

WARS AND RUMORS OF WARS

Next, Jesus said (Matt. 24:6,7; Mk. 13:7; Lk 21:9,10):

And you shall hear of wars and rumors of wars. See that you be not troubled; for all these things must come to pass, but *the end is not yet*. For nation shall rise against nation and kingdom against kingdom.

When Jesus gave this prophecy, it seems the Roman Empire was experiencing a general peace within its borders. But Jesus said they would be hearing of wars and commotions. And they did! Within a short time the Empire was filled with strife, insurrection, and wars.

Before the fall of Jerusalem, four emperors came to violent deaths within the space of 18 months. According to the historian Suetonius, Nero "drove a dagger into his throat." Galba was run down by horsemen. A soldier cut off his head and "thrusting his thumb into the mouth," carried the horrid trophy about. Otho "stabbed himself" in the breast. Vitellius was killed by slow torture and then "dragged by a hook into the Tiber." Writing of this period, the Roman historian Tacitus used such expressions as: "disturbances in Germany," "commotions in Africa," "insurrections in Gaul," "intrigues among the Parthians," "the war in Britain," "war in Armenia."

Among the Jews, the times became turbulent. In Seleucia, 50,000 Jews were killed. There was an uprising against them in Alexandria. In a battle between the Jews and Syrians in Caesarea, 20,000 were killed. During this period, Caligula ordered his statue placed in the temple at Jerusalem. The Jews refused and lived in constant fear that the emperor's armies would be sent into Palestine. The fear was so real that some of them did not even bother to till their fields.

But though there would be wars and commotions, Jesus told the disciples: "See that you be not troubled: for all these things must come to pass, but the *end* is not yet." Sermons are sometimes preached about deceivers, wars, rumors of wars, and other things mentioned in the opening portion of Matthew 24, as though they were signs of the soon coming of Christ! As a young preacher, not knowing any better, I did the same. But instead of these things being signs of the end, Jesus said: "The end is *not* yet"! Wars and commotions are of a general nature and, as such, could provide no definite sign that the end was at hand.

Something else that should be noticed is this: the word "end" here is not the same Greek word used in the expression "end of the world." (See footnote on page 48). Considering the setting, Barnes is no doubt correct when he says the end here is "the end of the Jewish economy; the destruction of Jerusalem."

FAMINES, PESTILENCES, EARTHQUAKES

Next, all three of the gospel writers, record the words of Jesus regarding "famines, and pestilences, and earthquakes in divers places" (Matthew 24:7; Mark 13:8; Luke 21:11).

The Bible tells about famine "throughout all the world...in the days of Claudius Caesar" (Acts 11:28). Judea was especially hard hit. "The disciples, every man according to his ability, determined to send relief unto the brethren which dwelt in Judea" (verse 29), taking up collections of food for the saints there (1 Corinthians 16:1-5; Romans 15:25-28). Historians such as Suetonius mention famine during those years. Tacitus speaks of a "failure in the crops, and a famine consequent thereupon." Eusebius mentions famines during this time in Rome, Judea, and Greece.

Along with famines, Jesus mentioned pestilence; that is, plagues, the spread of disease, epidemics. Famine and pestilence, of course, go hand in hand. Suetonius wrote of pestilence at Rome in the days of Nero which was so severe that "within the space of one autumn there died no less than 30,000 persons." Josephus records that pestilences raged in Babylonia in 40 A.D. Tacitus tells of pestilences in Italy in 66 A.D.

During this period, Jesus said there would also be earthquakes in many places. Tacitus mentions earthquakes at Rome, that "frequent earthquakes occurred, by which many houses were thrown down" and that "twelve populous cities of Asia fell in ruins from an earthquake." Seneca, writing in the year 58 A.D., said: "How often have cities of Asia and Achaea fallen with one fatal shock! how many cities have been swallowed up in Syria! how many in Macedonia! how often has Cyprus been wasted by this calamity! how often has Paphos become a ruin! News has often been brought us of the demolition of whole cities at once." He mentions the earthquake at Campania during the reign of Nero. In 60 A.D., Hierapolis, Colosse, and Laodicea were overthrown. Pompeii was greatly damaged by earthquake in 63 A.D. There were earthquakes in Crete, Apamea, Smyrna, Miletus, Chios, Samos, and Judea.

PERSECUTION AGAINST THE DISCIPLES

Jesus warned that for his name's sake, the disciples would be afflicted, hated, imprisoned, beaten, killed, brought before rulers and kings, but they would speak wisdom that their enemies could not gainsay or resist (Matthew 24:9; Mark 13:9-13; Luke 21:12-17). That such persecutions came upon the followers of Christ in those years is well known. They faced "great persecution" (Acts 8:1) and were "imprisoned and beat in every synagogue" (Acts 22:19). When called upon to answer charges, they were given wisdom that their persecutors could not resist (Acts 6:9,10). They were hated and some were put to death (Acts 7:59; 12:2).

Adding to the chaos, Jesus revealed that "many false prophets shall rise, and shall deceive many" (Matthew 24:11). Peter, who was one of the disciples present when Jesus gave this prophecy, later wrote about "false prophets" that had risen and of "many" that followed their pernicious ways (2 Peter 2). John, who also heard Jesus give this prophecy, recorded the fulfillment: "Many false prophets are gone out into the world" (1 John 4:1). Paul spoke of "false apostles, deceitful workers" (2 Corinthians 11:13). Hymenaeus and Philetus taught false doctrines and overthrew the faith of some (2 Timothy 2:17,18). By the time Paul wrote to Titus, there were "many...deceivers...who subvert whole houses, teaching things which they ought not" (Titus 1:10,11).

The waters of truth were muddied by betrayals, false prophets, iniquity, and the love of many waxing cold. "But he that shall endure [such things] unto the end, the same shall be saved" (Matthew 24:13)—both now and hereafter. We understand "end" here in a *general* sense, for unlike the use of this word in verses 6 and 14, this reference does not have the definite article in the Greek text.

GOSPEL TO BE PREACHED TO THE NATIONS

"And this gospel of the kingdom shall be preached in all the world for a witness unto all nations; and then [not until then] shall the end come" (Matthew 24:14). Unless we take this verse clear out of its setting, "the end" in view here is the end or destruction of Jerusalem.[1] This was the

---

[1] When the disciples spoke of "the *end* of the world" (Matthew 24:3), the word is *sunteleia* (Strong's Concordance, 4930). But in verses 6 and 14, the word translated "end" is *telos* (Strong's Concordance, 5056). Not realizing this, some have taken "end" in verses 6 and 14 to mean the end of the world. But the primary end in these verses, understood in context, would be the destruction of Jerusalem. Later, when Jesus answered the question about the end of the world, he used the term "that day"—when "heaven and earth shall pass away."

question that Jesus was answering in the verses before, and the verses that follow are still speaking about Jerusalem and Judea. Jerusalem would be destroyed, but "first" the gospel would be preached unto all nations (Mark 13:10).

It was a tremendous prophecy. Picture the scene. Here on the mount of Olives, Jesus spoke these words to insignificant men. Who would have supposed that their names would become known around the world and that even in our day—almost 2,000 years later—the seeds of truth they planted would still be producing fruit? Who would have supposed their message would ever spread beyond that immediate area?

Such a vast preaching program unto all nations seemed almost impossible of fulfillment. But it was fulfilled, and in a very real sense the gospel did go to all nations before the destruction of Jerusalem in 70 A.D.!

It began on the day of Pentecost. There were present in Jerusalem "devout men, out of *every nation* under heaven" (Acts 2:5) who heard the gospel preached by Peter. Three thousand were converted and many of these, no doubt, returned to their various countries and shared the gospel. Later when persecution came against the church at Jerusalem, believers were scattered and "went every where preaching the word," throughout the regions of Judea and Samaria (Acts 8:1,4). Philip took the message to the city of Samaria with great results and was later directed to a high ranking government official from Ethiopia who was gloriously converted. It is believed this man took the message to the continent of Africa and many others were converted because of his influential testimony.

Peter took the message to the Gentiles at the house of Cornelius, an event that was a turning point in the missionary activities of the church (Acts 10, 11). Missionary work advanced rapidly. The message spread to Rome. By the time of Nero, the Christians had grown so numerous that they aroused the jealousy of the government. The story of the great fire in Rome in 64 A.D.—for which the Christians were falsely blamed—is well known. In writing to the Christians at Rome, Paul opens his epistle by saying, "Your faith is spoken of throughout

49

the *whole world*" (Romans 1:8). His closing words of this epistle speak of the gospel as having been "made known to *all nations*" (Romans 16:26).

Apparently this included even far away England. Newton says: "There is absolute certainty that Christianity was planted in this country in the days of the apostles, before the destruction of Jerusalem." Eusebius and also Theodoret inform us that the apostles preached the gospel in all the world and some of them "passed beyond the ocean to the Britannic isles." By the time Paul wrote his letter to the Colossians, he could say: "The gospel...is come unto you, as it is in *all the world*...the gospel which you have heard, and which was preached to *every creature* which is under heaven" (Colossians 1:6, 23). By 70 A.D., the gospel had gone forth to the world for a witness. No longer was God's message to man confined to one nation or race!

THE ABOMINATION OF DESOLATION

When Jesus spoke of the temple being destroyed, the disciples asked: "WHEN shall these things be? and WHAT SIGN will there be when these things shall come to pass?" (Luke 21:7). As we have seen, Jesus mentioned things of a general nature that would happen first. Now he gives a *specific* sign. When they would see "the abomination of desolation," they would know the destruction of the city was "nigh." Upon seeing this, they were to flee quickly into the mountains.

Matthew: "When you therefore shall *see* the *abomination of desolation*, spoken of by Daniel the prophet, stand in the holy place, (whoso readeth, let him understand:) then let them that be in Judea flee into the mountains" (Matthew 24:15,16).

Mark: "When you shall *see* the *abomination of desolation*, spoken of by Daniel the prophet, standing where it ought not, (let him that readeth understand,) then let them that be in Judea *flee* to the mountains" (Mark 13:14).

Luke: "When you shall *see* Jerusalem compassed with *armies*, then know that the *desolation* thereof is nigh. Then let them which are in Judea *flee* to the mountains...Jerusalem shall be trodden down of the Gentiles" (Luke 21:20-24).

Notice now, step by step, the information contained in these parallel accounts.

1. Where Matthew and Mark record: "When you shall see the abomination of DESOLATION...then let them which be in Judea flee into the mountains," Luke says: "When you see *Jerusalem* compassed with armies, then know that the DESOLATION thereof is nigh. Then let them which are in Judea flee to the mountains." What was to become a desolation, then, was Jerusalem.

We notice also that this "desolation" was that "which was spoken by Daniel the prophet." Turning to Daniel 9, we find the passage in which Daniel spoke of this destruction: "And the people of the prince that shall come shall *destroy* the city and the sanctuary" (Daniel 9:26). A comparison of the parallel accounts, the reference to Daniel's prophecy, and the fact that Jesus was answering questions about the destruction of Jerusalem—all show that what was to become a desolation was Jerusalem.

2. Looking again at the parallel accounts, we see that what Matthew and Mark refer to as the "abomination" that would make Jerusalem desolate, Luke (using plain language) shows this would be accomplished by armies —Gentile armies: "And when you shall see Jerusalem compassed with *armies*, then know that the *desolation* thereof is nigh....Jerusalem shall be trodden down of the Gentiles" (Luke 21:20-24).

"Abomination" is a word that refers to anything that is especially loathsome or detestable. Certainly this fits the feelings the Jewish people would have toward idol-worshipping Gentiles, intent on destruction, taking a stand against their city.

3. Matthew's account says the abomination (Gentile army) would "stand in the holy place" and adds the words: "Whoso readeth, let him understand." Mark's account, because it too is given in somewhat veiled language, includes the words: "Let him that readeth understand." *But*, Luke's account of the same passage is given in *plain* language: "When you see Jerusalem compassed with armies..." Luke gives the *explanation;* and so, it should be carefully noted, does *not* include the phrase: "Let him that readeth understand."

By comparing scripture with scripture, we see that the term "holy place" (Matthew 24:15) refers to Jerusalem. This word usage is not inappropriate, for this portion is based on what was spoken by Daniel, and Daniel referred to Jerusalem as the "holy mountain" and "holy city" that was to become "desolate" (Daniel 9:16,24-27). Even after Jesus was rejected there, Jerusalem was still commonly referred to as the holy city (Matthew 27:53).

The word translated "place" in the expression "holy place" in Matthew's account is *topos* (Strong's Concordance, number 5117). It means simply a locality—words such as topical and topography are derived from it. It is used in such scriptural expressions as "a desert place," "dry places," etc. It is *not* the same term as used to describe the holy of holies of the temple.

What is called the holy place is explained by Luke as the area that would be occupied by armies surrounding Jerusalem. The *Matthew Henry Commentary* has well put it: "Jerusalem was the holy city, Canaan the holy land, the Mt. Moriah, which lay about Jerusalem, for its nearness to the temple was, they thought, in a particular manner holy ground; on the country lying round about Jerusalem the Roman army was encamped, that was the abomination that made desolate."[1]

These Gentile armies were to "compass" the city (Luke); they would take a "stand" there (Matthew). The word *stand* indicates rebellion or hostility, as the following examples show: "A king of fierce countenance...shall *stand* up" (Daniel 8:23,25). "A mighty king shall *stand* up, that shall rule with great dominion" (11:3). Another will "*stand* up in his estate, and shall come with an army" (verse 7). "Then shall *stand* up...a raiser of taxes...and in his estate shall *stand* up a vile person" (verses 20,21). A king "shall be stirred up to battle with a very great and mighty army; but he shall not *stand*" (verse 25). This wording from the book of Daniel is weighty since Matthew 24:15 is clearly rooted in that which was "spoken by Daniel the prophet."

According to Jesus, Jerusalem was marked for destruction. But a few days after Jesus mentioned these things, he commissioned his disciples to wait *in this very city*—to be endued with power from on high. They were to be witnesses unto him throughout the world, *including Jerusalem*, where their work would begin (Acts 1:8; Luke 24:49). But if the city was to be destroyed, what about those disciples who would be there for a witness? Were they to perish with the others—with those who rejected Christ and cried, "Crucify him, crucify him"? Or would there be a way of escape? According to the scriptures, their witness in that city was to continue up to a certain point—only until they saw a certain sign—and then they were to flee!

As is well known, the city of Jerusalem and the temple were destroyed by Roman armies in 70 A.D. But before this happened, in obedience to the warning Jesus had given, *every Christian fled* and thus escaped that disaster. The account of what happened is truly amazing!

In 65 A.D., Florus, the worse of Caesar's procurators, assumed control of Judea and aggravated the Jews to the point of rebellion—a rebellion too great for him to handle. Consequently, another man, Cestius Gallus, took over. Marching his armies into Palestine, he subdued a number of towns and advanced toward Jerusalem. After camping for three days near the city, he began the assault.[2]

Seeing Jerusalem compassed with armies, the disciples now knew its desolation was near—according to the words of Christ. This was their sign to flee! But *how* could they flee when the city was surrounded? This had not been explained in the prophecy. But notice what happened.

A WAY OF ESCAPE

When Cestius would have almost taken the city, suddenly, as Josephus says, "without any reason in the world," he withdrew his troops and departed! The Jews, who were about to open the gates in surrender, were now filled with courage as they pursued the retreating army, inflicting on it a major disaster.[3] With this retreat, there was a brief interval before the armies would return with reinforcements and destroy the city. In this interval, there was time for those who believed in Christ to flee. What happened is well summed up in the words of Thomas Newton:

We learn from ecclesiastical histories, that at this juncture *all* who believed in Christ departed Jerusalem, and removed to Pella and other places beyond the river Jordan; so that they all marvelously escaped the general shipwreck of their countrymen; and we do not read anywhere that so much as one of them perished in the destruction of Jerusalem.[4]

Adam Clarke wrote: "It is very remarkable that not a single Christian perished in the destruction of Jerusalem though there were many there when Cestius Gallus invested the city."[5] Truly it was a marvelous escape! What confirmation of our Lord's words! What an amazing fulfillment of prophecy!

After Cestius Gallus had retreated with his troops, Nero ordered Vespasian to take over. He, in turn, ordered his son, Titus, to go to Alexandria and bring the fifth and tenth legions from Egypt to subdue Judea. But a crisis in Rome caused Vespasian to return there (where he was hailed as the new Emperor in 70 A.D.). Meanwhile the job of capturing Jerusalem was left in the hands of Titus who brought about its destruction.[6]

In the place where Matthew and Mark use the somewhat veiled expression "abomination of desolation," Luke (using plain language) shows this would be Gentile armies compassing Jerusalem to bring it to desolation. This interpretation is solidly built on the Bible. With it, the gospel accounts are complementary, not contradictory. It is confirmed by history. It glorifies Christ, for it plainly demonstrates how his words were fulfilled and his warning heeded—thus providing a great deliverance and blessing for the Christians of that time!

THE FUTURIST INTERPRETATION

Having set forth what we believe to be the exact and only fulfillment of our Lord's words, we will consider the now-popular FUTURIST interpretation—that the "abomination of desolation" will be an idol placed in the holy of holies of a rebuilt Jewish temple. As one book expresses it: "The Jews—who will have...restored Herod's Temple, and be in league with Antichrist—will have a visit by the False Prophet who shall bring an image of the Antichrist into Jerusalem and wheel it into the temple....When this image

54

of the Antichrist is taken into the Jewish temple, that will be the sign Jesus mentioned in Matthew 24, the Abomination of Desolation."[7] Another says: "This image will be placed in the Jewish temple in Jerusalem, and is the 'abomination of desolation' to which the Lord made reference in his Olivet discourse"[8]—"an idol placed in the holy of holies of the temple during the reign of Antichrist."[9]

Though there are fine men of God who believe this way—and we do not want to treat lightly their ministries —we will point out what we feel are serious objections to this view.

1. The setting up of an idol in the holy of holies is something the enemy could not do until such a time as the temple would be in the enemies' possession. Since the magnificent temple would be the last thing yielded to an enemy in battle, by this time the city would have *already been captured*. It would probably be too late for Christians to flee then! An effective sign to warn Christians to flee would need to come *before* the capture of the city, not afterward!

2. The prophecy indicates that the "abomination" would destroy Jerusalem and the temple—would make desolate. This is exactly what the Roman armies did. But with the teaching that the "abomination" will be an idol set up in the temple, there is contradiction. How could the abomination be an idol set up in the temple, when the temple was to be destroyed *by* the abomination? Idols are abominable, of course, but they are not desolators!

3. The "abomination" that would make desolate was to be something that could be *seen* by the inhabitants of Judea and Jerusalem. "When you *see* the abomination"; that is, "when you *see* Jerusalem compassed with *armies*," then, "let them that are in Judea flee into the mountains." It is evident that Jesus was not talking about an idol in the holy of holies, for such could not be seen by the population of Jerusalem and Judea. Only the high priest entered the holy of holies. None of the ordinary Jews would dare enter there.

The futurist interpretation regarding the abomination of desolation requires a rebuilt temple in Jerusalem. Some, in fact, even offer this as proof that the temple *will be re-*

built. The reasoning goes something like this: Since the "abomination of desolation" will involve the inner sanctum of the temple, "it is certain that the Temple will be rebuilt. Prophecy demands it."[10] We see no demand for such, for what temple was the subject of Matthew 24 and the parallel accounts? Was Jesus talking about *that* temple of his day or a *rebuilt* temple 2,000 years later?

It is evident Jesus spoke of the temple of his day; he talked about the stones which it contained, had the disciples look at it, and answered questions about it! Are we to assume that he was not actually speaking of that temple at all, but of a rebuilt temple—a different temple, a temple made of different stones, a temple to be built 2,000 years later? We believe the answer is evident.

Whether the Jewish people will build another temple in Jerusalem is not the issue. The point is that Jesus was speaking of the temple of his day and it was that temple which was to be destroyed by heathen armies—a prophecy which was fulfilled in 70 A.D.

The disciples asked when the temple would be destroyed and what sign would be given in warning. "And Jesus *answered...*"—he told them *when,* he gave them a *sign*—as we have seen. But those who think the prophecy of Matthew 24 refers to a *future* temple are at a complete loss to show one verse in this chapter where Jesus ever answered these questions!

The teaching that the abomination of desolation is something yet future, not only requires a future and different temple, but such a temple—instead of being destroyed—is pictured as a place where the Antichrist will set up an idol for worship. If so, this would be a *preserved* temple—a shrine of false religion—not a *destroyed* temple. The prophecy of Matthew 24 and the parallel accounts never mention a future temple.

FLEE TO THE MOUNTAINS

There was an urgency in the message of Jesus about fleeing: "Then let them which be in Judea flee into the mountains; let him which is on the housetop not come down to take anything out of the house; neither let him which is in the field return back to take his clothes. And woe unto them that are with child, and to them that give suck in those days! But pray that your flight be not in the winter, neither on the sabbath day" (Matthew 24:16-20). The parallel accounts say the same.

Those who would heed the warning of Jesus were to flee without delay. They were not to try to take their possessions with them. Such actions might have been questioned and their escape hindered. They were told to pray their flight would not be in winter lest the elements delay and hinder; neither on the sabbath. Making their escape on the sabbath, could have easily brought them into suspicion by those who held that only a short distance (at a slow pace) could be traveled on that day. Naturally, there would also be problems for those with small children.

The area from which they were to flee was Judea and especially Jerusalem. They were to flee into the mountains. The setting is definitely Palestine, and the time—as indicated by the prophecy itself, as well as the historical fulfillment—was back in the *first century!*

But popular prophecy books like *The Late Great Planet Earth*, make statements like: "The residents of Israel who believe in Jesus will flee to the mountains and canyons of Petra for divine protection,"[11]—as though what Jesus mentioned is still in the future! And why to *Petra?* The Bible does not say this. William Blackstone, in 1935, even sent workers to Petra where they placed Hebrew Bibles (encased in copper boxes) in some of the caves in that area. He believed the Jews would flee there during the tribulation period and read his Bibles!

Futurism commonly takes verses that were fulfilled long ago, and applies them to some current event. I recall a sensational sermon title of the 1950s: "The A-BOMB-ination of Desolation," supposedly linking the words of Jesus with the desolation caused by atomic bombs!

A booklet in my possession says that Matthew 24 refers to "atomic warfare," that safety will only be found in the mountains for those in Judea, and that when they flee to the mountains, they should not take their clothing because it will be "dangerously radio active." The "woe" to those with child and that give suck, is taken to mean atomic explosions will make mothers' milk "harmfully radio active." The verse that says, "Pray that your flight be not in winter, neither on the sabbath day," is interpreted to mean that weekends, especially in winter, will be times of the greatest danger. It is pointed out that Hitler chose weekends for his big surprises and that the Japanese did so at Pearl Harbor. Finally, the writer says: "If a surprise attack comes, therefore, it is most likely to be on a weekend. It would be good insurance to be particularly well prepared at such times, especially in winter"![12]

In all due respect to fine men who have taught such things, we must say that only by taking this passage out of its context and by minimizing (or ignoring) the historical fulfillment, can these words be thus applied. Why were the disciples given a sign to flee into the mountains prior to 70 A.D.? The passage goes on to explain.

THEN SHALL BE GREAT TRIBULATION

For then shall be *great tribulation*, such as was not since the beginning of the world to this time, no, nor ever shall be. And except those days should be shortened, there should no flesh be saved: but for the elect's sake those days shall be shortened (Matt. 24:21,22; Mk. 13:19,20).

Luke's account says: "For these be the days of *vengeance*, that all things which are written may be fulfilled...for there shall be *great distress* in the land [Judea], and *wrath* upon this people [the Jews]. And they shall fall by the edge of the sword, and shall be led away captive into all nations: and Jerusalem shall be trodden down of Gentiles..." (Luke 21:22-24).

Unless we completely ignore the setting, it is evident that the tribulation mentioned here is that which was to come upon the people of Jerusalem and Judea—tribulation that would result in the destruction of their city and temple. General things such as wars, famines, pestilence, and earthquakes would occur, none of which would be the specific sign of the impending desolation. But when they would see Jerusalem compassed with armies, then they would know the desolation was near. This would be the sign to flee into the mountains. "For then shall be *great tribulation.*"

58

Josephus, the Jewish historian, was an eye-witness to the unparalleled tribulation that ended in the fall and destruction of Jerusalem in 70 A.D. His detailed and scholarly account, *Wars of the Jews*, was published about 75 A.D., while the events of which he wrote were still fresh in the memory of thousands. His history provides a marvellous confirmation of the prophecy Jesus gave, even

JOSEPHUS

to fine details. Since he was not a Christian, no one can accuse him of slanting his material to match the prophecy. The references we will give in the account that follows are from Josephus.

The trouble in Jerusalem began over differences between the Jews and the Romans. There were also differences between Jews—some favored a revolt against Roman rule, others hoped for a peaceful agreement. Those who favored revolt became very violent and began to kill those who disagreed with them. Troops were sent in to control the mob. War was on! Not only at Jerusalem, but throughout the land there was unrest.

"Every city was divided into two armies," Josephus says, "and the preservation of the one part was in the destruction of the other; so the daytime was spent in shedding blood, and the night in fear—which was of the two the more terrible....It was then common to see cities filled with dead bodies, still lying unburied; those of old men mixed with infants, all dead and scattered about together; women also lay amongst them, without any covering for their nakedness: You might then see the whole province full of *inexpressible calamities* while the dread of still more barbarous practices which were threatened, was everywhere greater than what had been already perpetrated."[13]

The Jews in Alexandria that revolted against the Romans "were destroyed *unmercifully;* and this, their destruction, was complete...houses were first plundered of what was in them, and then set on fire by the Romans; wherein no mercy was shown to the infants, and no regard had to the aged; but they went on in the slaughter of persons of every age, till all the place was overflowed with blood, and fifty thousands of them lay dead upon heaps."[14]

In one hour, over 20,000 were killed in Caesarea and the battle continued until "all Caesarea was emptied of its Jewish inhabitants....Galilee was all over filled with fire and blood, nor was it exempted from any kind of misery or calamity."[15] Such *horror* was in the land that one prominent man, in order to save his family from a worse fate, took a sword and killed first his aged father and mother, his wife and children—all submitting to it willingly—and then took his own life.[16]

In Jerusalem, those of the revolting party were known as Zealots. They "fell upon the people [who disagreed with them] as upon a flock of profane animals, and *cut their throats.*" In this way, 12,000 of the more eminent inhabitants perished. "The terror that was upon all the people was so great, that no one had courage enough either to weep openly for the dead man that was related to him, or bury him...those that mourned for others soon underwent the same death with those whom they mourned for."[17]

Slaughter continued until "the outer temple was all of it overflowed with blood, and that day they saw 8,500 dead bodies there." Included in this number were "those that a little before had worn the sacred garments and presided over the public worship, which were cast out naked to be the food of dogs and wild beasts." Even those who came with sacrifices were slain, "and sprinkled that altar...with their own blood; till the dead bodies of strangers were mingled together with those of their own country, and those of profane persons with those of priests, and the blood of all sorts of dead carcasses stood in lakes in the holy courts themselves."[18]

"The noise also of those that were fighting was incessant, both by day and by night; but the lamentations of those that mourned exceeded the other...their calamities came perpetually, one upon another....But for the seditious themselves, they fought against each other, while they trod upon the dead bodies as they lay heaped one upon another, and taking up a mad rage from those dead bodies that were under the feet, became the fiercer thereupon...and when they had resolved upon anything, they executed it without mercy, and omitted no method of torment or of barbarity."[19]

No wonder Jesus said: "Daughters of Jerusalem, weep not for me, but for yourselves, and for your children" (Luke 23:28)—knowing that all these things would come upon that generation! Many Jews were killed *by Jews*, not by the enemy outside the walls. Josephus says the Jews "never suffered from the Romans anything worse than they made each other suffer." Such madness shows the validity of Jesus' words when he likened that generation to a man possessed of demons (Matthew 12:43-45).

Food became scarce within the walls of the city. Many of the Jews, venturing out by night to search for food, were caught, "tormented with all sorts of *torture*," and then crucified in the sight of those on the walls. About 500 every day were thus killed until the number finally became so great that there was not room enough for the crosses, nor

JOSEPHUS PLEADS WITH THE JEWS TO SURRENDER.

enough crosses for the victims. Often several were nailed to the same torture stake. Imagine the torment of those who would see or hear of their loved ones being thus tortured a short distance from the walls. Many had their hands cut off.[20]

"Then did the famine widen its progress, and devoured the people by whole houses and families; the upper rooms were full of women and children dying by famine; and the lanes of the city were full of the dead bodies of the aged; a kind of deadly night, had seized upon the city....Thus did the miseries of Jerusalem grow worse and worse every day...the multitude of carcasses that lay in heaps one upon another was a horrible sight, and produced a pestilential stench."[21]

"The number of those that perished by famine in the city was prodigious, and their miseries were unspeakable. For if so much as the shadow of any kind of food did anywhere appear, a war was commenced presently, and the dearest friends fell fighting one another about it....Children pulled the very morsel that their fathers were eating, out of their very mouths, and what was still more to be pitied, so did the mothers do to their infants: and when those that were almost dead were perishing under their hands, they were not ashamed to take from them the very last drops that might preserve their lives....

"The seditious...also invented terrible methods of torment to discover where any food was, and they were these: to stop up the passage of the privy parts of the miserable wretches, and to drive sharp stakes up their fundaments! and a man was forced to bear what it is terrible even to hear."[22]

One woman of prominence killed and roasted her infant son. When she had eaten half, she hid the other half. When certain seditious Jews smelled the scent of roasted flesh, they threatened to cut her throat if she did not show them where it was. She then uncovered the remaining half of the little body, saying: "Come, eat of this food; for I have eaten of it myself! Do not you pretend to be either more tender than a woman, or more compassionate than a mother." But even those hardened men, horrified at the sight, left the house trembling.[23]

Surely these things fulfilled the prophetic warning given years before: "The Lord shall bring a nation against thee from far...which shall not regard the person of the old, nor show favor to the young....And thou shalt eat the fruit of thine own body, the flesh of thy sons and of thy daughters....The tender and delicate woman among you, which would not adventure to set the sole of her foot upon the ground for delicateness and tenderness, her eye shall be evil toward...her young one...and toward her children...for she shall eat them for want of all things secretly in the siege and straitness, where with thine enemy shall distress thee" (Deuteronomy 28:49-57).

Some, attempting to escape from the city, swallowed pieces of gold in order to take them unnoticed. Once this was known, soldiers cut them open searching for gold. "Nor does it seem to me that any misery befell the Jews that was more terrible than this, since in one night about 2,000 of these deserters were thus dissected." [24]

BURNING OF THE TEMPLE

Finally the Roman armies broke through the wall and an enraged soldier caught the temple on fire. "While the holy house was on fire, everything was plundered that came to hand, and ten thousand of those that were caught were slain; nor was there a commiseration of any age, or any reverence of gravity; but children, and old men, and profane persons, and priests, were all slain in the same manner....The flame was also carried a long way and made an echo, together with the groans of those that were slain...nor can one imagine anything either greater or more terrible than this noise...one would have thought that the hill itself, on which the temple stood, was seething-hot, as full of fire on every part of it." [25] As the temple burned, the Jews knew all hope for deliverance was gone. The aqueducts and city sewers were crowded as the last place of refuge for the hopeless. When these were searched, two thousand people were found dead there, and those still alive were dragged out and killed.

Highly significant is the fact that the very date on which the temple was burned by the armies of Titus, was the same date that Nebuchadnezzar had burned it centuries before! "But, as for that house, God had for certain long ago doomed it to the fire, and now that fatal day was come, according to the revolution of the ages; it was the tenth day of the month Ab, upon which it was formerly burnt by the king of Babylon"![26]

The scriptures had warned: "And the Lord shall bring you into *Egypt* again with ships, by the way whereof I spake unto thee, Thou shalt see it no more again: and there you shall be sold unto your enemies for bondmen and bondwomen, and no man shall buy you" (Deuteronomy 28:68). Josephus tells how those that survived were led away captives, some being taken into *Egypt!* "As for the rest of the multitude that were above 17 years old, he put them into bonds, and sent them to the Egyptian mines...and sold the rest of the multitude with their wives and children, and every one of them at a low price, and that because such were sold were very many, and the buyers few."[27]

The accompanying illustration is of a Roman medal which was struck to commemorate the capture of Jerusalem. The side shown at the top, pictures Titus and gives his titles in abbreviated Latin. The reverse side has letters which mean "Captive Judea." By a palm tree, a Jewish woman is weeping and a man stands with hands tied behind his back.

There were 97,000 that were sold as slaves and 1,100,000 people that perished during the tribulation of those days, "the greater part of whom were indeed of the same nation, but not belonging to the city itself; for they were come up from all the country to the feast of unleavened bread, and were suddenly

shut up by an army....The multitude of those that therein perished exceeded all the destruction that either men or God ever brought upon the world." [28]

Josephus wrote: "I shall therefore speak my mind here at once briefly:—that neither did any other city suffer such *miseries*, or did any age ever breed a generation more fruitful in *wickedness* than this was, *from the beginning of the world.*"[29] The calamities which befell the Jews were "the *greatest* of all those, not only that have been in our times, but, in a manner, of those that *ever* were heard of; both of those wherein cities have fought against cities, or nations against nations...it appears to me that the misfortunes of all men, from the beginning of the world, if they be compared to these of the Jews, are not so considerable as they were."

In a footnote, the Christian translator of Josephus' works adds this comment: "That these calamities of the Jews, who were our Savior's murderers, were to be the *greatest* that had ever been since the beginning of the world, our Savior had directly foretold (Matthew 24:21; Mark 13:19; Luke 21:23,24) and that they proved to be such accordingly, Josephus is here a most authentic witness."[30]

"There have been, of course, other periods of tribulation or suffering in which greater numbers of people were involved, and which continued for longer periods of time," writes Boettner. "But considering the physical, moral, and religious aspects, suffering never reached a greater degree of awfulness and intensity than in the siege of Jerusalem. Nor have so many people ever perished in the fall of any other city. We think of the atomic bomb that was dropped on Hiroshima as causing the greatest mass horror of anything in modern time. Yet only about one-tenth as many people were killed in Hiroshima as in the fall of Jerusalem. Add to the slaughter of such a great number the bestiality of Jews to Jews and of Roman to Jews and the anguish of a people who knew they were forsaken of God, and we see the justification for Christ's words, 'For then shall be great tribulation, such as hath not been from the beginning of the world until now, no, nor ever shall be!'"[31]

When Jesus spoke of tribulation "such as was not since the beginning of the world...nor ever shall be," he was using a *proverbial* form of expression. Similar expressions are found in various ways in the scriptures: "...before them there were no such locusts as they, neither after them shall be such" (Exodus 10:14). "I will give thee [Solomon] riches, and wealth, and honor, such as none of the kings have had that have been before thee, neither shall there any after thee have the like" (2 Chronicles 1:12). "...there was none like thee before thee, neither after thee shall any arise like unto thee" (1 Kings 3:12). "I will do in thee that which I have not done, and whereunto I will not do any more the like" (Ezekiel 5:8,9). "...a great people...there hath not been ever the like, neither shall be any more after it, even to the years of many generations" (Joel 2:2). "A time of trouble, such as never was since there was a nation even to that same time" (Daniel 12:1).

Some might argue there have been greater times of tribulation since 70 A.D. They could also argue that there have been kings who have had more wealth and honor than Solomon. But seeing how this expression was used in the scriptures, we should not attempt to press it beyond its intended meaning. We believe the historical fulfillment fully meets the requirements of the prophecy about great tribulation and wrath upon that land and people.

An arch was erected in Rome to commemorate the victory of Titus and the Roman armies in the destruction of Jerusalem. Seven hundred of the Jewish captives were reserved by Titus to follow the carriage in which he made his triumphal entry into Rome. Carried in the procession were the spoils taken from the temple—the golden table, the seven-

branched candlestick, the veils of the sanctuary, and the book of the law. Over the centuries, this monument that portrays these things has been a witness to the fulfillment of Jesus' words concerning the tribulation that came upon Jerusalem and Judea.

Knowing the intensity of that tribulation, Jesus had prophesied:

> And except those days should be shortened, there should no flesh be saved [alive]; but for the elect's sake those days shall be shortened (Matt. 24:22; Mark 13:20).

We must bear in mind that the reference here is to the area upon which the tribulation of those days fell—Judea and Jerusalem. It should not be wrested from its proper setting.

Concerning judgment that fell upon this *same* land in the Old Testament, we read: "Your country is desolate, your cities are burned with fire: your land, strangers devour it in your presence, and it is desolate....Except the Lord of hosts had left unto us a very small remnant, we should have been as Sodom, and we should have been like unto Gomorrah" (Isaiah 1:1,7,9). In the cities of Sodom and Gomorrah, of course, no flesh was saved alive. It was total destruction.

There is an obvious *similarity* here. In the Old Testament, "except the Lord" had left a remnant, no flesh would have been saved alive. In the New Testament, "except the Lord" had shortened the days, no flesh would be saved alive. The meaning is basically the same in both cases. It is not necessary to read atomic bombs and modern times into this passsage. Josephus informs us that "the populace was *almost annihilated*...there was no part of Judea, which did not partake of the calamities of the capital city."

Though the Christians had escaped into the mountains, living without housing or provisions, they too could have eventually been destroyed by sword or famine. For their sake those days were shortened. God had placed definite, foreordained limits: "Jerusalem shall be trodden down of the Gentiles [the Roman armies] until the times of the Gentiles [the Roman armies] be fulfilled" (Luke 21:24).

Some pull these five words, "The times of the Gentiles," out of their setting and attempt to stretch them far into the *future*. Ironside has written that this is "the entire period during which the nation of the Jews, the city of Jerusalem, and the land of Palestine are under Gentile domination. This began with Nebuchadnezzar's conquest of Palestine and will end at the Revelation of the Lord Jesus Christ from heaven at the close of the Great Tribulation."[32] This is Scofield dispensationalism.[33] We see no scriptural basis for this. Figuring from the time Vespasian received his commission from Nero and declared war on Jerusalem (February, 67 A.D.) until the end of the siege and destruction of the city and temple (August, 70 A.D.), this treading down of Jerusalem—in actual time—was three and a half years.

SUN, MOON, AND STARS DARKENED

"Immediately after the tribulation of those days, shall the sun be darkened, and the moon shall not give her light, and the stars shall fall from heaven, and the powers of the heavens shall be shaken" (Matthew 24:29).

Luke's account says: "There shall be signs in the sun, and in the moon and in the stars; and upon the earth distress of nations with perplexity; the sea and the waves roaring; men's hearts failing them for fear, and for looking

68

after those things which are coming on the earth [the *land*]; for the powers of heaven shall be shaken" (Luke 21:25,26).

We have before us now a description of the condition of things after the tribulation.** Are we to understand these expressions about the darkening of the sun, moon, and stars literally or figuratively? We believe Jesus used these expressions the same way the Old Testament prophets did: figuratively. They commonly used these expressions to describe various disasters: the sun shall go down, sun darkened, light darkened in the heavens, no light in the heavens, the moon shall not give her light, stars shall fall, stars darkened, cloudy day, darkness at noon day, etc.

While such language was more common to the eastern world and ancient times, yet even today we might describe the future as "bright" or "dark," depending on circumstances. We commonly speak of the "Dark Ages." When a person sees a truth or fact clearly, we say he saw the "light." An intelligent person is "bright." People who are outstanding in the entertainment field are called "stars."

In Joseph's dream, his father, mother, and brothers were symbolized by the sun, moon, and stars (Genesis 37:9-11). Wording about falling stars was used to describe the calamities that fell upon the Jews in the days of Antiochus Epiphanes (Daniel 8:10). Stars symbolized the messengers of the seven churches (Revelation 1:16,20). In hieroglyphic writing, the sun, moon, and stars were used as symbols—representing empires, states, kings—and the darkening of the heavenly bodies symbolized the overthrow of empires, states, and rulers.

The nation of Israel, when obedient, was promised *bright* days (blessings): "He shall bring forth thy righteousness as the LIGHT, and thy judgment as the NOON DAY" (Psalms 37:6). "Then shall thy LIGHT break forth as the morning...then shall thy LIGHT RISE in obscurity, and thy darkness be as the NOON DAY" (Isaiah 58:8-10). "Thy SUN

---

* *Strong's Concordance*, 3625.
** That the tribulation referred to is the *same* as the one mentioned previously, there is no doubt. Jesus said there would be great tribulation and except "*those* days" were shortened no flesh would be saved alive. And then we read: "...immediately after the tribulation of *those* days." Mark's account says: "But in those days, after *that* tribulation..."

69

shall no more go down; neither shall thy MOON withdraw itself: for the Lord shall be thine everlasting LIGHT, and the days of thy mourning shall be ended" (Isaiah 60:20).

On the other hand, when disobedient, Israel was warned of dark days (trouble, judgment): "We wait for light, but behold OBSCURITY; for brightness, but we walk in DARKNESS...we stumble at noon day as in the night" (Isaiah 59:9,10), a day of "DARKNESS, and *not* light...even very DARK, and no brightness in it" (Amos 5:18-20). "The end is come upon my people of Israel...I will cause the sun to go down at noon, and I will DARKEN the earth in the clear day" (Amos 8:2,9).

This same type of wording was used to describe the destruction that came upon Egypt: "Thus saith the Lord God; I will also make the multitude of Egypt to cease by the hand of Nebuchadnezzar, king of Babylon. He and his people...shall be brought to destroy the land...the day shall be DARKENED...a cloud shall cover her, and her daughters shall go into captivity" (Ezekiel 30:6-18). "And when I shall put thee out, I will cover the SUN with a cloud, and the MOON shall not give her light. All the bright lights of heaven will I make DARK over thee, and set DARKNESS upon thy land...I shall bring thy destruction...I shall make the land of Egypt desolate" (Ezekiel 32:2-15).

The same type of wording was used to describe the destruction that came upon Idumea. "And all the *hosts of heaven* shall be dissolved and the heavens shall be rolled together as a scroll; and all their hosts shall fall down...for my sword shall come down upon Idumea...from generation to generation it shall lie waste" (Isaiah 34:4-10).

In the prophecy regarding the fall of Babylon, which was to come "as destruction from the Almighty," we read: "He shall destroy the sinners thereof out of it. For the STARS of heaven and the constellations thereof shall not give their light: the SUN shall be darkened in his going forth, and the MOON shall not cause her light to shine....Behold, I will stir up the *Medes* against them...and Babylon...shall be as when God overthrew Sodom and Gomorrah" (Isaiah 13:9-21). The fulfillment of this prophecy is evident. The kingdom was given to that ancient people known as the Medes (Daniel 5:28-31). This was not an end-of-the-world-prophecy, even though it was described in language about the sun, moon, and stars being darkened.

The same type of wording was used concerning the Old Testament destruction of Jerusalem: "I will also stretch out my hand upon Judah, and...Jerusalem...a day of wasteness and desolation, a day of DARKNESS and gloominess, a day of clouds and thick DARKNESS" (Zephaniah 1:4,15). "And if one look unto the land, behold DARKNESS and sorrow, and the LIGHT is darkened in the heavens thereof" (Isaiah 5:3,30). "I beheld...the heavens, and they had no LIGHT...the heavens above were BLACK" (Jeremiah 4:3,23,28). Jeremiah warned them to turn to God in repentance "before he cause DARKNESS, and...while you look for LIGHT, he turn it into the shadow of death, and make it gross DARKNESS" (Jeremiah 13:9,10,16-19). "Therefore NIGHT shall be unto you...it shall be DARK...the SUN shall go down...the day shall be DARK over them...Jerusalem shall become heaps" (Micah 3:6,12).

When Babylon was overthrown by the Medes and others, it was not the *literal* sun, moon, and stars that were darkened. When Idumea became a desolation, it was not the *literal* stars of heaven that were dissolved. When Egypt and Jerusalem were overthrown and became desolate under the attack of Nebuchadnezzar, it was not the *literal* sun, moon, or stars that were darkened. These expressions symbolized *very dark times* for these various places. Now, if the Lord saw fit to use these symbols in the Old Testament, why should we suppose he would use different terms when he became flesh and dwelt among us?

As we have seen, the prophecy of Jesus about the tribulation pertained to a certain city—Jerusalem; to a certain land—Judea; to a certain people—the Jewish nation. What would be the condition of things for that city, nation, and people "immediately after the tribulation of those days"? Would they experience only a passing tribulation after which things would return to normal? No! Transferring the expression about the darkened sun, moon, and stars from symbol to fact, the picture is that of a complete overthrow, destruction, desolation! This interpretation is solidly built upon the scriptures and its accuracy is confirmed by history.

And then shall appear the sign of the Son of man in heaven; and then shall all the tribes of the earth mourn; and they shall see the Son of man coming in the clouds of heaven with power and great glory. And he shall send his angels with a great sound of a trumpet, and they shall gather together his elect from the four winds, from one end of heaven to the other (Matthew 24:30,31; Mark 13:26,27; Luke 21:27,28).

It would seem we have before us now a description of the second coming of Christ. For this reason, futurists start here and work backward through Matthew 24. By this method they place the tribulation, abomination of desolation, earthquakes, famines, pestilences, and wars as end-time events. But in so doing, the very foundational theme of the prophecy—the destruction of the temple —must be ignored.

The arguments for the fulfillment of everything in Matthew 24 up to this point are so sound, some believe, and argue at length, that the coming of the Lord *did* occur at this time—resurrection, rapture, and all—in 70 A.D.[34] The weakness of this position is the lack of any history to confirm it. It tends to leave us hanging.

Others feel the Lord came figuratively or spiritually in 70 A.D.—to judge Jerusalem. In a sense this is true, for the Father has given Christ all authority to execute judgment (John 5:22-27), which would have included his judgment upon Jerusalem, when he "sent forth his armies and destroyed those murders, and burned up their city" (Matthew 22:7). According to Josephus, a strange omen appeared at that time: "I suppose the account of it would seem to be a fable, were it not related by those that saw it, and were not the events that followed it of so considerable a nature as to deserve such signals; for, before sunsetting, chariots and troops of soldiers in their armor were seen running about among the clouds."[35] Were these angels? Was this a sign of Christ coming in judgment upon Jerusalem?

Even though there will be the final great and glorious coming of Christ, it is certainly true he sometimes comes in other ways for blessing or judgment: *"Return O Lord,* unto the many thousands of Israel" were words of a prayer when the ark was set up and rested (Numbers 10:36). After the captivity at Babylon, God said, "I am *returned* unto Jerusalem" (Zechariah 1:16; 8:3). The Lord *came* to men in dreams (Genesis 20:3). He *came down* to see the city (Genesis 11:5). "I am *come down* to deliver thee" out of Egypt (Exodus 3:8). "Lo I *come* unto thee in a thick cloud" (Exodus 19:9). The Lord "riding upon a swift cloud," came into Egypt (Isaiah 19:1). "The Lord...bowed the heavens ...and *came down*...he delivered me" (Psalms 18:6-17). No one understands these verses as references to the second coming of Christ.

Being so closely associated with the apocalyptic language about darkened sun, moon, and stars, it is not impossible that the coming of the Son of man in the clouds (in Matthew 24:30,31) could be understood in the same way. But this is not without problems of interpretation. With this view, the sending forth of angels with the sound of a trumpet to gather the elect, is taken to mean sending the apostles to preach the gospel whereby people could be gathered into the church. But even granting that the word translated "angels" can be translated "messengers," we would normally think of the apostles being sent forth at the ascension of Jesus, not his return. By 70 A.D. these men had *already* gone forth into all the world with the gospel.

Because of many second coming verses about angels coming with Christ, believers being gathered unto him, the sound of the trumpet, etc., we favor the interpretation which applies Matthew 24:30,31 to the return of Christ in power and glory at the end of this age. Of course this raises an objection. In verse 29, we read about the condition of things "immediately after the tribulation of those days." And this next verse says: "And *then*...they shall see the Son of man coming in the clouds of heaven with power and great glory." Would this not indicate that the second coming was to occur right then? It would seem so. However, the word "then" (used by Matthew more than all other New Testament writers put together) can mean an event will happen right away, *or* it can indicate the *order* in which events will happen. Applied in this latter sense, we could understand Matthew 24 in this way: Jesus spoke of general events that were to occur before the overthrow of Jerusalem and then the specific sign of that destruction: Gentiles armies surrounding Jerusalem. The invading armies would bring about great tribulation for the people left in Jerusalem and Judea. The condition of things immediately after that tribulation would be that of desolation. All of these things would happen first, "and then"—in the order of events mentioned—"shall appear...the Son of man coming in the clouds of heaven with power and great glory." Our explanation will not satisfy everyone, but an appeal to other verses seems to justify this position.

1. The second coming was not to be at the fall of Jerusalem, for Jesus expressly warned about any who would say that Christ had come in those days—and was in the desert or in some secret place (Matthew 24:23-27).

2. Jesus said Jerusalem would be destroyed and the Jews who were not killed in the tribulation would be led captive into all nations (Luke 21:24). This could not be the same time as the second coming of Christ at the end of the age, for Jews will not be led away captive into all nations then. It was following the events of 70 A.D. that they were led away captive. The one event was the end that came upon Jerusalem; the other will be the end of the age.

3. In a later part of Matthew 24, Jesus expressly said that no man knows the time of the second coming, the end of the age (Matthew 24:35,36). But concerning the overthrow of Jerusalem, Jesus knew the time and stated it would be *before* that generation then living would pass away. They had asked *when* this destruction would be, and he told them. But the time of the second coming was *not* revealed. There is a distinct contrast here. The possibility that a long period of time might pass before the coming of Christ is suggested by the story of the bridegroom that did not appear until the midnight hour or the master who "after a long time" returned (Matthew 25:5,6,19).

4. The destruction of Jerusalem was preceded by a specific sign—Jerusalem compassed with Gentile armies. But the second coming will be "as a thief in the night"; we are exhorted to be ready at all times; there will be no specific sign (such as a huge cross in the sky) to warn people a few minutes before Christ returns. People will be eating

74

and drinking and getting married—the routine things, just as in Noah's day—and will not be expecting anything unusual to happen. Suddenly Christ will come! The sign preceding the fall of Jerusalem was specific; the signs or warnings about the second coming are general—nothing to reveal the day or hour!

5. At the time of the fall of Jerusalem, the disciples were to escape into the mountains. Then, there was time to flee; but when Christ comes there will be no time to flee or make preparations to meet him. At the second coming, believers will not flee into the mountains, but will be caught up to meet the Lord in the clouds. In the first century, they *scattered*; at the second coming they will be *gathered.* It is contrast all the way through.

THE FIG TREE

Now learn a parable of the fig tree; when his branch is yet tender, and putteth forth leaves, you know that summer is nigh: so likewise, when you shall see all these things, know that it is near, even at the doors. Verily I say unto you, *This generation* shall not pass, till all these things be fulfilled (Matthew 24:32-34; Mark 13:28-30).

Futurists, seeking to place Matthew 24 in modern times, teach that the blossoming fig tree refers to Israel becoming a nation in 1948. "When the Jewish people, after nearly 2,000 years of exile, under relentless persecution, became a nation again on 14 May 1948 the 'fig tree' put forth its first leaves,"[36] writes Hal Lindsey in 1970. He goes on to suggest, figuring a generation as 40 years, that all would be fulfilled by 1988. But subtract from this seven years—according to the dispensational view—and the rapture would have taken place in 1981! The passing of time has now shown both dates to be erroneous.

It is commonly assumed there are numerous Biblical references about the fig tree being a symbol of Israel. But looking into the Old Testament, there is little—if any—evidence for this.

In the New Testament, there are two references about fig trees that are sometimes regarded as symbolizing Israel. In the one, a parable, the owner of the fig tree came for "three years" seeking fruit on the tree and found none. When he ordered that the tree be cut down, the gardener suggested that they let it remain another year, and—if it remained unfruitful—to then cut it down (Luke 13:6-9). If the fig tree here symbolizes Israel, this would show how Israel lacked the fruits of repentence, even after Christ had come to them and ministered for over three years.

The other fig tree reference is Matthew 21:19. But here, again, the reference is not to a fruitful tree, but to an unfruitful tree, a tree that Jesus cursed: "Let no fruit grow on thee henceforward for ever." There are no other verses that indicate the fig tree is a symbol of Israel. On the other hand, there are verses that refer to Israel as an OLIVE tree (Romans 11:17,24).

ALL THE TREES!

But returning to Jesus' statement about the fig tree, we need look no further than the text itself to find full proof that he was *not* talking about the nation of Israel! Matthew's account says: "Now learn a parable of the fig tree; when his branch is yet tender, and putteth forth leaves, you know that summer is nigh..." But Luke's account shows that Jesus did not single out only *one* tree in this illustration. "Behold the fig tree, AND ALL THE TREES: when they now shoot forth, you see and know of your own selves that summer is now nigh at hand" (Luke 21:29). If the fig tree represents the nation of Israel, then "all the trees" would have to represent all the nations. With this, the passage would have no point at all! In view of this, Dake (though a dispensationalist) has well said: "The fig tree...is universally interpreted to mean the Jewish nation, *but this could not possibly be the meaning.*"[37]

Jesus was merely drawing an illustration from nature. He said that when the fig tree and all the trees put forth leaves, people recognize that summer is near. It was a comparative statement, not unlike saying that when the sun is in the west, we know that night is at hand; when snow is on the ground, we know it is winter time; when the leaves turn color, we know it is autumn; when we see dark clouds gathering, we know it is going to rain. Jesus used a simple, comparative illustration—something they could know of themselves. It was human knowledge that when trees put forth leaves, men know that summer is at hand; so likewise, when they would see "all these things" come to pass, such would be a sign to them.

What did Jesus mean by "all these things"? He had just spoken of the second coming. Was this a continuation of what he had just spoken, or was he here returning to the original line of thought? If we take it to refer to everything that Jesus had just said, the passage would have to read something like this: "When you see the sun darkened, the moon not giving her light, the stars falling, the powers of heaven shaken, the sign of the Son of man in heaven, all tribes mourning, the Son of man coming in the clouds, the trumpet sounding, the angels gathering the elect from around the world: when you see all these things you will know the coming of the Lord is near, even at the doors." This could not be what he meant.

We believe he was returning to the *original* line of thought—the things that would lead up to the destruction of Jerusalem: deceivers, wars, famines, pestilences, earthquakes, and finally the specific sign—Jerusalem compassed with Gentile armies. When they would see all *these things*—they would know the destruction of Jerusalem was near. The proof that it was to "these things" that Jesus referred, is found in the statement that follows:

> Verily I say unto you, *This generation* shall not pass till all these things be fulfilled (Matthew 24:34; Mark 13:30; Luke 21:32).

Jesus had said one stone would not be left upon another that would not be thrown down—Jerusalem and its temple were marked for destruction. The disciples asked: "*When* shall these things be?" Here, then, was his answer! These things would happen before the generation then living would pass away. Living on this side of the fulfillment, we know that these things did happen within the time specified. It is an amazing fulfillment of prophecy!

Just before Matthew 24, in chapter 23, Jesus had warned that generation of Jews: "Fill up then the measure of your fathers....Behold, I send unto you prophets, and wise men...some of them you shall kill and crucify; and some of them shall you scourge in your synagogues, and persecute them from city to city: that upon you may come all the righteous blood shed upon the earth, from the blood of righteous Abel unto the blood of Zacharias son of Barachias, whom you slew between the temple and the altar. Verily I say unto you, *all these things* shall come upon THIS GENERATION. O Jerusalem, Jerusalem....Behold, your house is left unto you desolate" (Matthew 23:32-38).

In commenting on this passage, Scofield very correctly says: "It is the way also of history: judgment falls upon one generation for the sins of centuries. The prediction was *fulfilled* in the destruction of Jerusalem, A.D. 70."[38] *But*, a few verses later, in Matthew 24, when Jesus said: "This generation shall not pass, till all these things be fulfilled"—a statement which would place the great tribulation back then—Scofield tries to make "generation" mean "race, kind, family, stock, breed"! Then, based on this definition, concludes: "The promise is, therefore, that the generation—nation, or family of Israel—will be preserved unto 'these things'."[39]

MEANING OF "GENERATION"

But as we go through the book of Matthew, we can see by context how Jesus used the word generation. First, there is Matthew 1:17: "So all the generations from Abraham to David are fourteen generations...." This reference is not to 14 different races, but to fourteen different generations of that race—each generation following the other in logical sequence. Jesus asked: "Whereunto shall I liken this generation?"—a reference to that generation then living. Jesus called it "an evil and adulterous generation," and likened it to a man possessed of demons whose latter end was worse than the first. The people of Nineveh "shall rise in judgment with this generation, and shall condemn it" (Matthew 12:38-45). It was a "faithless and perverse generation" (Matthew 17:17).

Then in Matthew 23, Jesus reproved the hypocrisy of that generation and said they were no better than their fathers (former generations) that had killed the prophets; judgment upon Jerusalem was certain; their house would be left desolate—"all these things shall come upon this generation" (Matthew 23:36). Finally, Matthew 24:34: "This generation shall not pass, till all these things be fulfilled."

We feel it is arbitrary to take "generation" in all these other places in Matthew to mean the generation living at one time, and then in Matthew 24 try to make it mean the whole race of Jews over a period of 2,000 years or more! Only to uphold a theory would anyone do this.

Strangely enough, those who say "generation" means the Jewish people as a *race* in Matthew 24, also say the Jewish race will *never* pass away. So if Jesus meant the Jewish race will not pass away until these things are fulfilled, and if the Jewish race will never pass away, his words were meaningless. But taking the word "generation" in its normal and primary meaning—the generation of people living at one time—Jesus did indeed answer the question: "WHEN shall these things be?"

THE END OF THE AGE

Heaven and earth shall pass away, but my words shall not pass away. But of *that day* and hour knoweth no man, no, not the angels of heaven, but my Father only (Matthew 24:35,36; Mark 13:31,32).

To this, Luke's account adds:

And take heed to yourselves lest at any time your hearts be overcharged with surfeiting and drunkenness, and cares of this life, and so *that day* come upon you unawares. For as a snare shall it come (Luke 21:33-35).

Up to this point, Jesus spoke of things leading up to and including the destruction of Jerusalem. Two times he briefly left his original line of speech to contrast those events with the second coming (Matthew 24:27,30-31). After telling of things that would happen in that generation, the whole discourse now shifts to the question about the second coming and the end of the world. Jesus said that heaven and earth shall pass away—the end of the age—and that the time of "that day" is not revealed.

Then shall two be in the field; the one shall be taken and the other left. Two women shall be grinding at the mill; the one shall be taken and the other left. Watch therefore, for you know not what hour your Lord doth come (Matthew 24:40-42).

Dispensationalists who suppose these verses describe a pre-tribulation rapture, face serious difficulties of interpretation. We are clear down at verse 40. To harmonize with the dispensational outline, these verses should have been back in the early part of Matthew 24—before the tribulation, before the abomination of desolation, before the flight into the mountains! But no hint of a secret rapture is found anywhere in those early verses. Not until *"after* the tribulation"—regardless of how we understand the tribulation of Matthew 24—do we read of the Lord's coming when one will be taken and the other left!

BIBLICAL REFERENCES FOR "TRIBULATION"

The word that is translated "tribulation" in Matthew 24 is *thlipsis* (Strong's Concordance, 2347). This Greek word is sometimes translated affliction, anguish, persecution, burdened, and trouble. A study of all references in which this word appears may be summed up in the following categories:

First, *tribulation upon the Jews*. As we have seen, Jesus spoke of "great tribulation" (Matthew 24:21). Luke's account says: "There shall be great distress in the land" —Judea—"and wrath upon this people"—the Jews—"and Jerusalem shall be trodden down of the Gentiles" (Luke 21:23,24). We know this tribulation came to its end in 70 A.D.

Second, *tribulation against Christians*. "In the world you shall have tribulation" (John 16:33). "We must through much tribulation enter into the kingdom" (Acts 14:22). "Tribulation worketh patience" (Romans 5:3). Tribulation shall not separate us from Christ (Romans 8:35-37). We are to be "patient in tribulation" (Romans 12:12), "joyful in all our tribulations" (2 Corinthians 7:4), and faint not at tribulation (Ephesians 3:13; 2 Thessalonians 1:4). In the book of Revelation, the church at Smyrna suffered tribulation (Revelation 2:9,10). John, the writer of Revelation, refers to himself as "your brother and companion in tribulation" (Revelation 1:9). This type of tribulation spans the entire gospel age.

One portion of Revelation describes a vision of the redeemed—multitudes out of all nations—who "came out of great tribulation" (Revelation 7:14). Some point out that the Greek text has "the" in front of the words "great tribulation" in this verse—*"the* great tribulation." Immediately some suppose this is an end-time tribulation period of seven years. But this is faulty reasoning, for the Greek text also has "the" in Revelation 1:9: "I John, your brother, and partaker with you in *the* tribulation." John was suffering tribulation back in the *first century*—the tribulation—and the whole gospel era has been marked with tribulation for Christians in one place or another, in one way or another.

When John saw the vision of the "great multitude which no man could number," he was told they came out of the great tribulation, or, as some translate it, they came *through* great tribulation. It does not say they came out *before* the tribulation. Even dispensationalists, though they believe in a pre-tribulation rapture of the church, do not see the rapture here. They believe these are *tribulation* saints, "the greatest number of converts in all history" (as Hal Lindsey says), who will be converted *after* the rapture! Why some believe that people who "miss the rapture" will win more souls in seven years, than faithful and obedient Christians who were ready for the rapture, is difficult to figure out.

Unwittingly, our dispensational brothers have come up with a new formula for success in the ministry! Assuming the rapture will take place *soon*, a man who desires a successful, soul-winning ministry could make certain he is *not* ready for the rapture. By missing the rapture, he could then repent, preach during the tribulation period, and be numbered among the greatest soul winners of all time!

Third, *tribulation upon the wicked.* To the Thessalonian believers who were enduring "persecutions and tribulations" (2 Thessalonians 1:4), Paul wrote: "It is a righteous thing with God to recompense tribulation to them that trouble you" (verse 6). *When?* "When the Lord Jesus shall be revealed from heaven with his mighty angels, in flaming fire taking vengeance on them that know not God...when he shall come to be glorified in his saints" (verses 7-10). Here Christ comes with the angels, in flaming fire, taking vengeance on the wicked. This is also when he comes to be glorified in his saints. There is no *secret* rapture here!

Even if there were two stages to the second coming, this could not be the first stage.

Dispensational writers commonly argue that the rapture will occur before the "Tribulation Period," because God has not appointed Christians to wrath: "The church of Jesus Christ has never been destined to suffer the pangs of the Tribulation Period....Scripture: 'For God hath not appointed us [who are born again] to wrath' (1 Thessalonians 5:9)."[40] But what "wrath" is this verse talking about? Notice the *context.*

When Christ descends from heaven, believers will be caught up to meet him in the air, and "sudden destruction" will fall upon the wicked "and they shall not escape." It is *concerning this wrath*—not a seven year tribulation period—that we read: "For God hath not appointed us to wrath, but to obtain salvation by our Lord Jesus Christ" (See 1 Thessalonians 4:16-5:9). Christians are not appointed to wrath, but only a few verses before Paul *did* say they are appointed to tribulation! "No man should be moved by these afflictions [*thlipsis*—tribulations]: *for* yourselves know that we are *appointed* thereunto. *For* verily...we told you before that we should suffer *tribulation*" (1 Thessalonians 3:3,4).

JACOB'S TROUBLE

One prophecy remains to be considered here—the time of Jacob's trouble. "Alas! for that day is great, so that none is like it: it is even the time of *Jacob's trouble,* but he shall be saved out of it" (Jeremiah 30:7). Because this description uses the terms "great" and mentions trouble "so that none is like it," dispensationalists assume this refers to a final seven year tribulation period. And since this "is the time of Jacob's trouble, *not the church's,*" it is further assumed the church will be raptured *before* this time![41] But such conclusions can hardly be justified when taken in context.

Because the book of Jeremiah is a long book—the second longest in the Bible—many are not familiar with the setting in which this prophecy was given. Jeremiah repeatedly warned the Israelites that enemy armies would come against them; they would be taken into captivity; they would be punished by God—if they did not repent. They did not repent, and the time of trouble came upon them. They were taken into captivity by the king of Babylon. However, the prophecy said: "But he [Jacob—Israel] shall be saved out of it." This happened when God allowed the people to return from the Babylonian captivity.

We have heard a voice of *trembling*, of *fear*, and not of *peace*. Ask ye now, and see whether a man doth *travail* with child? wherefore do I see every man with his hands on his loins, as a woman in *travail*, and all faces are turned into paleness? Alas! for that day is great, *so that none is like it:* it is even THE TIME OF JACOB'S TROUBLE; but he shall be *saved* out of it. For it shall come to pass in that day, saith the Lord of hosts, that I will break his *yoke* from off thy neck...I will *save* thee from afar, and thy seed from the land of their *captivity;* and *Jacob shall return*...I will bring again the captivity of Jacob's tents...and the city shall be builded upon her own heap (Jeremiah 30).

1. The prophecy about Jacob's trouble mentioned "a voice of *trembling*" (verse 5). Was this the case when the king of Babylon came against them? Yes. "We have sinned against the Lord. We looked for peace...and for a time of health, and behold trouble! The snorting of his horses was heard...the whole land *trembled*" (Jeremiah 8:14-16).

2. Jacob's trouble would be a time of *fear* (verse 5). Did fear come upon the people in those days? Yes. "Behold, a people cometh from the north country...they ride upon horses....We have heard the fame thereof: our hands wax feeble...*fear* is on every side" (Jeremiah 6:22-26). "*Fear* and a snare is come upon us, desolation and destruction" (Lamentations 3:47).

3. The prophecy said *peace* would be taken from them (verse 5). Was their peace taken away in those days? Yes. "I have taken away my *peace* from this people....We looked for peace...and behold trouble" (Jeremiah 8:15; 16:5).

4. The prophecy likened Jacob's trouble to the *travail* of a woman with child. This also happened. "What will thou say when he shall punish thee?...sorrows shall take thee as a woman in *travail*" (Jeremiah 13:21). "Pangs have taken thee as a woman in *travail*...for now shalt thou go forth out of the city...even to Babylon" (Micah 4:9,10).

83

5. It would be a time of *trouble* so *"that none is like it"* (verse 7). Does this properly describe the trouble that came upon that people? Yes! Ezekiel, using language very similar to that of Jeremiah, said: "Thus saith the Lord...I am against thee, and will execute judgments in the midst of thee...I will do in thee *that which I have not done, and whereunto I will not do any more the like,* because of all thine abominations" (Ezekiel 5:8,9). When this punishment came upon them, Jeremiah said it was *"greater* than the punishment of the sin of Sodom, that was overthrown as in a moment" (Lamentations 4:6). Daniel wrote of that time of trouble in these words: "All Israel have transgressed thy law...therefore the curse is poured upon them ...God hath confirmed his words, which he spake against us...by bringing upon us a great evil: for under the whole heaven *hath not been done as hath been done* upon Jerusalem" (Daniel 9:11,12). Such proverbial wording was used by the prophets to describe times of trouble that were uniquely severe (see pp. 65, 66).

6. Though this time of trouble would come upon Jacob, the prophecy said: "He shall be *saved* out of it...I will *save* thee from afar, and thy seed from the land of their captivity; and Jacob shall *return*" (Jeremiah 30:7,10). They had the promise that "after seventy years be accomplished at Babylon, I will visit you...in causing you to *return*...I will turn away your captivity...I will bring you again into the place whence I caused you to be carried away captive" (Jeremiah 29:10-14). "I am with you to save you" (Jeremiah 42:11). "Fear not thou, O my servant Jacob...I will *save* thee from afar...Jacob shall *return*" (Jeremiah 46:27).

The details of the return from the seventy year captivity at Babylon are spelled out in the book of Ezra.

Here, then, we have the prophecy about Jacob's trouble and deliverance, complete with other scriptures that record the fulfillment, often in precisely the same wording. It all fits together. But some have set all of this aside, supposing this prophecy is still future, because of the closing words: "...in the *latter* days you shall consider it" (Jeremiah 30:24). Reading the expression "the latter days" it is easy to assume the very end of *this* age is intended. But the word *latter* (which is used several times in

84

Jeremiah) simply expressed an undefined future—"in the future" or "*later on* you will consider it."

When these things had all happened, they were able to "consider" or understand the fulfillment of what had been prophesied. In this case, the "latter" days were those days *after their captivity*. The house of God that they built upon their return was the *"latter* house" as compared to the *"former"* house before the captivity (Haggai 2:9). After their return, the prophets that had warned them before the captivity were referred to as "the *former* prophets" (Zechariah 1:4; 7:7,12) which would mark the days after the captivity—in comparison—as the *later* or *latter* days. It is in this sense that the expression is used in Jeremiah 30. What Jeremiah called "the time of Jacob's trouble" is now ancient history—not an end-time tribulation period!

SEVEN YEAR TRIBULATION PERIOD?

With so much talk in some Christian circles about a future seven year Tribulation Period—and all the discussion as to whether the rapture will be pre-trib or post-trib—it is amazing that one simple fact has been commonly overlooked: There is *not one verse* anywhere in the entire New Testament that mentions a seven year tribulation period!

Are we implying there will be no tribulation at the end of the age? All through the centuries there have been times of tribulation experienced by Christians—to one degree or another. We have no guarantee that the last days will be any exception. But we do not believe there will be the type of tribulation period that is commonly presented in dispensational circles.

The Bible teaches that at the time of the second coming, the end of the age, people will be eating and drinking, marrying and giving in marriage, planting and building, buying and selling (Luke 17:26-30). Accordingly, things will be continuing in what will be considered a normal, routine pattern. People will be saying, "Peace and safety" (1 Thessalonians 5:3). But if "all hell will break lose" upon the earth in the way some have proclaimed, surely after undergoing this for seven years, people would not be saying, "Peace and safety."

Writing a number of years ago, Guinness has well said:

> If such signs as are imagined by some were to precede the advent, the state of society predicted in these passages could not by any possibility exist. If monstrous, unheard of, supernatural, portentous events were to transpire, would they not be telegraphed the same day all over a startled world, and produce such a sense of alarm and expectation that buying and selling, planting and building, marrying and giving in marriage, would all be arrested together, and 'peace and safety' would be far from anyone's lips?[42]

In view of these things, we conclude there will not be the type of tribulation that some have envisioned during the last years of this age. But no one has every detail figured out, it is no time for arrogance or dogmatism. We don't know the day or the hour of Christ's return. The important thing is to watch and be ready at all times, "looking for the blessed hope, and the glorious appearing of the great God and our Savior Jesus Christ" (Titus 2:13).

* * * * * * * * * * * *

The section of this book which follows will begin with the amazing prophecy of Cyrus and a discussion concerning the proper starting point of the seventy weeks prophecy. Then we will take up the question: Is the seventieth week *future* or *fulfilled?* This question will be especially significant in connection with what we have seen, for the whole idea that there will be a great tribulation of *seven years* duration is based on the teaching that the seventieth week is yet future.

Part Three:

DANIEL'S SEVENTIETH WEEK
—Future or Fulfilled?

It was a scene of despair for the Israelites who were captives in Babylon. Their city, Jerusalem, had been destroyed (2 Chronicles 36:15-21). Many of their young men, including Daniel, had been castrated and forced to serve in the king's palace (2 Kings 20:18; Daniel 1:6-8). The discouragement of the people is reflected in Psalm 137:1-4: "By the rivers of Babylon, there we sat down, yea, we wept, when we remembered Zion. We hanged our harps upon the willows in the midst therefore. For they required of us a song, saying, Sing us one of the songs of Zion. How shall we sing the Lord's song in a strange land?"

But then hope broke through. By a study of certain "books," Daniel determined that the length of the captivity would be 70 years, a period that was now almost over. Then, by divine intervention, they would be set free to return and build their city of Jerusalem. As Daniel thought on these things, the angel Gabriel came to him and spoke of another time period—seven times as long—70 weeks (of years). He explained that the 70 weeks (69 of which would measure unto Messiah!), were to be counted from the going forth of "the commandment to restore and to build Jerusalem" (Daniel 9:25). In the portion that follows, we will take a close look at this great prophecy of the 70 weeks, but for now we must focus on certain details that mark the *beginning* of this prophetic measurement.

We read that "Daniel understood by *books* the number of years, whereof the word of the Lord came to Jeremiah the prophet, that he would accomplish seventy years in the desolations of Jerusalem" (Daniel 9:2). Turning to the book of Jeremiah, we can read, as Daniel did, this same prophecy: "Thus saith the Lord, That after *seventy years* be accomplished at Babylon, I will visit you, and perform my good word toward you, in causing you to return" (Jeremiah 29:10; 25:11). Other details about the deliverance that was to come were given in the book of Isaiah, which was also, as we shall see, among the "books" that Daniel studied. The prophecy in Isaiah is especially significant, for it revealed the *name* of the man that would set the captives free and cause Jerusalem to be built again. His name would be CYRUS.

> Thus saith the Lord to his anointed, to Cyrus, whose right hand I have holden, to subdue nations before him; and I will loose the loins of kings, to open before him the two leaved gates; and the gates shall not be shut; I will go before thee, and make the crooked places straight...I will give thee the treasures of darkness, and hidden riches of secret places...he shall build my city, and he shall let go my captives, not for price nor reward, saith the Lord (Isaiah 45:1-3, 13).

Cyrus has been mentioned by various historians of antiquity. Herodotus says the Persians regarded him highly;

Ammianus calls him "the amiable prince" of the Oriental world; Xenophon lauds the wisdom by which he governed; Plutarch declares that in wisdom and virtue he surpassed all kings. Cyrus is mentioned by name in the Bible 23 times. The accompanying drawing shows the way Cyrus is pictured on an ancient monument.

Amazingly, the prophecy in Isaiah regarding Cyrus, was revealed *150 years before Cyrus was born!* "Thus saith the Lord...of CYRUS, He is my shepherd, and shall perform all my pleasure: even saying to Jerusalem, Thou shalt be built; and to the temple, Thy

"CYRUS THE GREAT"—*Ridpath's History of the World.*

foundation shall be laid....Thus saith the Lord to CYRUS...I call thee *by name*...I have surnamed thee, though thou hast not known me" (Isaiah 44:24,28-45:1-4).

This one that God called by name would be the one who would allow the captives to return. "I will direct all his ways: he shall build my city, and he shall *let go my captives*, not for price nor reward, saith the Lord" (Isaiah 45:13). But before Cyrus could ever be in a place of authority to fulfill this prophecy, it is evident that Babylon, which held the Jews captive, would have to be overthrown. This, from all natural reasoning, seemed impossible.

Historians such as Herodotus, Rawlinson, and Prideaux tell us that the city of Babylon was inclosed by a 60 mile wall estimated to be over 200 feet high and 87 feet

"OVERTHROW OF BABYLON"—*Ridpath's History of the World.*

thick. This in turn was surrounded by a moat of equal cubic capacity with the wall. The huge gates that provided entry to the city were made of solid brass. Passing through the middle of the city was the Euphrates river which was also lined with walls. The Babylonians figured their provisions within the city would last for 20 years and their gardens were capable of supplying food for an indefinite period of time. Consequently, when Cyrus began to lay siege to Babylon, they felt his efforts were useless. But in this feeling of security was the very source of their danger!

Learning of a great pagan festival that the Babylonians would be observing, Cyrus planned a surprise attack. On the night of the festival—when the inhabitants and king would be spending their time in revelry and drunkenness—he would channel the waters of the Euphrates (which ran beneath the walls and through the city) into a 40 square mile area which had been built for flood control. This being accomplished, with the lowering of the water, the armies of Cyrus would march through the river bed and beneath the outer walls!

With this in mind, it is interesting to notice that within the prophecy about Cyrus—though the language is veiled (as is often the case in prophecy)—we read: "Thus saith the Lord...to the deep, Be dry, and I will dry up thy rivers" (Isaiah 44:27).

After the armies of Cyrus had gotten within the main walls, however, there were still the walls along the river which would prevent their entrance into the city. In these walls, where streets crossed the river, were huge gates of brass which normally would have been closed and locked. But in the neglect and spell of the celebrations, *these gates had not been shut!* Now we can understand the significance of the words: "Thus saith the Lord...to Cyrus...I will open before him the two leaved gates; and *the gates shall not be shut*...I will break in pieces the gates of brass, and cut in sunder the bars of iron" (Isaiah 45:1,2). In other words, the way would be completely opened up for Cyrus. The obstacles would be removed. The gates and iron bars would, as it were, be broken and cut in sunder!

Meanwhile, what was happening inside the city is revealed in Daniel 5. King Belshazzar made a great feast —called 1,000 of the leaders of his kingdom—and together they drank wine and praised their gods. That night mysterious handwriting appeared on the wall and "the king's

THE HANDWRITING ON THE WALL.

91

countenance was changed, and his thoughts troubled him, so that the joints of his *loins were loosed*, and his knees smote one against another" (Daniel 5:6). Such was exactly what God had revealed he would do in preparing the way for Cyrus. "Thus saith the Lord to...Cyrus...I will *loose the loins of kings*" (Isaiah 45:1). Here we have a prophecy in Isaiah and the fulfillment in Daniel—described by the very same wording!

What did the handwriting on the wall mean? The wise men of Babylon could not explain it. Finally, Daniel was called and he explained it was a message of doom for the king and his kingdom, and that the kingdom would be given to the Medes and Persians.

At this very time, the armies of Cyrus were gaining entrance to the city. How timely was the message! "In that night was Belshazzar...slain. And Darius the Median took the kingdom, being about sixty two years old" (Daniel 5:30,31). Prideaux tells us that Darius was the uncle of Cyrus and "Cyrus allowed him the title of all his conquests as long as he lived."[1] After Darius died, however, *Cyrus* became the sole leader of the kingdom (Daniel 6:28).

In the prophecy to Cyrus, God said he would "subdue *nations* before him" (Isaiah 45:1). Did this happen? Yes! Here is a list of fourteen nations he conquered: the Cilicians, Syrians, Paphlagonians, Cappadocians, Phygians, Lydians, Carians, Phenicians, Arabians, Assyrians, Bactrians, Sacae, Maryandines, as well as the Babylonians.

Prophecy also revealed that God would cause Cyrus to receive "the *treasures* of darkness, and hidden *riches* of secret places" (Isaiah 45:3). It was the custom for a conquering king in those days to hide the treasures he took in battle, such not being used unless it became an absolute necessity. These were placed in the "treasure house" (cf. Daniel 1:2). In Babylon there were many such treasures —from Egypt, Assyria, Judea, and other countries that had been conquered. Such hidden treasures of the kingdom—even as the prophecy had said—became the property of the conquering Cyrus! According to Pliny, the silver and gold Cyrus took in would be worth $353,427,200 (figured in today's money), plus various other jewels, vessels, and precious things!

These great victories of Cyrus were an exact fulfillment of prophecy. Cyrus had now come to the position of leader in the kingdom—the position in which it would be his right to set the captives free. *But* for a worldly minded king—a hardened military man—to suddenly release thousands of his slaves "not for price nor reward" seemed *impossible!* Slaves meant wealth, fame, and prestige to any king. But one day Cyrus was stirred to "let them go"! Who has ever heard of such things? It is contrary to all natural reasoning. But this is what happened—and right on time!

When Cyrus proclaimed the freedom of these slaves, he also put it *in writing.* Copies of this official document are still available today. Would you like to read a copy of that proclamation? You can; it is right in your Bible!

> Now in the first year of Cyrus king of Persia, that the word of the Lord by the mouth of Jeremiah might be fulfilled [the prophecy which stated the captivity would last for 70 years], the Lord stirred up the spirit of Cyrus king of Persia, that he made a proclamation throughout all his kingdom, and put it also in writing, saying, Thus saith Cyrus king of Persia, the Lord God of heaven hath given me all the kingdoms of the earth; and he hath charged me to build him an house at Jerusalem [this was in the prophecy of Isaiah 44:28]....Who is there among you of all his people? his God be with him, and let him go up to Jerusalem, which is in Judah, and build the house of the Lord God... (Ezra 1:1-3; also 2 Chronicles 36:22,23).

The account of these things given by the Jewish historian Josephus confirms what we have already seen. One special point of interest is that Cyrus read his own name in the book of Isaiah. Knowing this was written 140 years before the temple was destroyed, and now another 70 years had also passed, he was stirred to action!

> In the first year of the reign of Cyrus, which was the seventieth from the day that our people were removed out of their own land into Babylon, God commiserated the captivity and calamity of these poor people, according as he had foretold to them by Jeremiah the prophet...that after they had undergone that servitude seventy years, he would restore them again to the land of their fathers, and they should build their temple....God stirred up the mind of Cyrus, and made him write this throughout all Asia: Thus saith Cyrus...God indeed foretold my name

by the prophets, and that I should build him a house at Jerusalem.' This was known to Cyrus by his reading the book which *Isaiah* left behind him of his prophecies...*one hundred and forty years before the temple was demolished.* Accordingly, when Cyrus read this, and admired the Divine power, an earnest desire and ambition seized upon him to fulfil what was so written; so he called for the most eminent Jews that were in Babylon, and said to them, that he gave them leave to go back to their own country, and to rebuild their city Jerusalem."[2]

KING CYRUS SIGNS THE DECREE PERMITTING THE JEWS TO RETURN FROM BABYLON AND REBUILD JERUSALEM.

Here, then, was "the going forth of the commandment to restore and to build Jerusalem"—the decree of Cyrus —marking the beginning of the 70 "weeks" prophecy which would measure unto Messiah. But according to the dates given by Ussher, this decree would be too early. Consequently, some have chosen the twentieth year of Artaxerxes (when letters were given to Nehemiah to go to Jerusalem) as the proper starting point of the 70 weeks prophecy.[3] But instead of seeking a later decree from that of Cyrus, we feel what should be questioned is the dating system commonly used for this period. Ussher, Lloyd, and others have all based their chronological conclusions on the canon of Ptolemy, a list of Persian kings and the length of time they reigned. But as Mauro says: "Ptolemy does not even pretend to have had any facts as to the length of the Persian period (that is to say, from Darius and Cyrus down to Alexander the Great)"; his dates are based on "calculations or guesses made by Erathosthenes, and on certain vague floating traditions."[4]

In 1913, Martin Anstey published a detailed and scholarly book, *Romance of Bible Chronology*, which contained a system of chronology far superior to any of the former systems.* By taking all verses in the Bible that mention a date, an age, or any chronological information, he thoroughly demonstrated that the Bible contains its own complete chronological system from Adam to the decree of Cyrus and on down to the time of Christ. By a variety of proofs, taken entirely from the scriptures, Anstey showed that the period which Ptolemy assigns to the Persian empire is about 80 years too long. Consequently, problems have resulted when men have tried to make Biblical events and dates harmonize with the calculations of Ptolemy.

Interestingly, though Dr. Scofield originally favored using the decree of Artaxerxes, when he read Anstey's book which upheld the decree of Cyrus as the correct starting point for the 70 weeks prophecy, he accepted this position and rejected the erroneous chronology of Ptolemy. This was pointed out in his book *What Do the Prophets Say?*, published in 1918. "Whatever confusion has existed at this point has been due to following the Ptolemaic instead of the Biblical chronology, as Anstey in his 'Romance of Bible Chronology'."[5] The dates were not corrected in the Scofield Bible notes, however.

---

*Anstey's work is out of print, but all basic points are included in Philip Mauro's *The Wonders of Bible Chronology*. Copies may be obtained from Ralph Woodrow, P. O. Box 21, Palm Springs, CA 92263-0021. Price: $7.00 including postage.

Those who reject the decree of Cyrus as the proper starting place for the 70 weeks, commonly present the argument that the proclamation of Cyrus had only to do with the rebuilding of the "house of God" (Ezra 1), whereas the 70 weeks were to begin with the commandment to build the *city.* Gaebelein, for example, says: "It is wrong to reckon these 70 year weeks from...the time Cyrus gave permission for the people to return and to build the temple...for they are to begin with the word to restore and build the city itself."[6]

It is true that the portion of the decree of Cyrus that is recorded in Ezra 1 mentions only the rebuilding of the temple and does not specifically mention the rebuilding of the city (houses, streets, walls, etc.) But since the temple would be the most unique building there, the construction of which could easily become a most controversial matter, it is not unnatural that it would be expressly and especially mentioned. However, we have no reason to believe that provision was not also made for the building of the city with houses and streets. Are we to suppose the people were to return and build a temple and yet have no place for themselves to live? Are we to suppose Cyrus would grant permission and support for the building of the temple (which was eventually decorated with gold and silver and contained rare vessels) and not make provision for a wall around the city to protect it? Edward Young has written:

> It is not justifiable to distinguish too sharply between the building of the city and the building of the temple. Certainly, if the people had received permission to return to Jerusalem to rebuild the temple, there was also implied in this permission to build for themselves homes in which to dwell. There is no doubt whatever but that the people thus understood the decree. The edict of Cyrus mentions the temple specifically, because that was the religious center of the city, that which distinguished it as the holy city of the Jews.[7]

According to Bible prophecy, *Cyrus* was to be the one who would speak the word which would cause the city of Jerusalem to be built, as well as the temple. "He [Cyrus] is my shepherd, and shall perform all my pleasure: even saying to JERUSALEM, Thou shalt be *built;* and to the

TEMPLE, Thy foundation shall be laid" (Isaiah 44:28). "I have raised him up in righteousness, and I will direct all his ways: *he shall build my city*, and shall let go my captives, not for price nor reward" (Isaiah 45:13). So also says Josephus: Cyrus gave leave to the Jews "to go back to their own country, and *to rebuild their city Jerusalem*, and the temple of God."[8] In a letter to governors in Syria, Cyrus wrote: "I have given leave to as many of the Jews that dwell in my country as please to return to their own country, *and to rebuild their city*, and to build the temple of God at Jerusalem on the same place where it was before."[9]

Turning now to the book of Ezra, let us look—chapter by chapter—at the actual history of what happened when the Jews returned.

Ezra, chapter *one* records the decree of Cyrus with special mention of the rebuilding of the temple. Chapter *Two* gives a list of those who returned. Chapter *Three* tells us that the "people gathered themselves together as one man to Jerusalem," built an altar, and made offerings, "but the foundation of the temple of the Lord was not yet laid" (verses 1,6). It was not until two years and two months later that the foundation of the house of the Lord was laid (verses 8-11). During this time they were probably building houses to live in.

Chapter *Four* tells of a letter in which their adversaries said: "...the Jews...are come unto Jerusalem, building the rebellious and the bad *city*, and have set up the *walls* thereof, and joined the foundations" (verses 11-16). Discouragement crept in and the work ceased on the house of God (verse 24).

Eventually, the prophets Haggai and Zechariah stirred them to action, as revealed in Ezra, chapter *Five*. "Then the prophets, Haggai...and Zechariah...prophesied unto the Jews" and work resumed on the house of God (verses 1,2). Haggai's message was this: "Is it time for you, O ye, to dwell in your *ceiled houses*, and this house lie waste?....Consider your ways...ye looked for much, and, lo, it came to little; and when ye brought it *home*, I did blow upon it. Why? saith the Lord of hosts. Because of mine house that is waste, and ye run *every man* unto his *own*

97

"REBUILDING JERUSALEM"—*Ridpath's History of the World.*

house" (Haggai 1:1-9). Did the returned captives build houses for themselves to live in? Did "every man" have his "own house"? The answer is obvious. They saw to it that *they* had houses to live in, but had put off further work on the house of *God.*

Ezra, chapter *Six,* tells about continued work on the house of God. When some challenged their right to build, a search was made in the "house of rolls [scrolls]" and the "decree" that had been issued by Cyrus was found. (It was no accident that Cyrus had put this in writing!) King Darius (this Darius being the son of Hystaspes) then issued a decree in which he confirmed the words of Cyrus. "And the elders of the Jews builded...and this house was *finished* on the third day of the month Adar, which was in the sixth year of the reign of Darius" (verses 14,15).

Ezra, chapter *Seven,* says: "Now after these things, in the...seventh year of Artaxerxes the king" (verses 1,7), Ezra was given a letter authorizing him to go to Jerusalem "and to carry the silver and gold, which the king and his counsellors freely offered unto the God of Israel" (verse 15). Ezra rejoiced because God had put it in the king's heart "to beautify the house of the Lord" (verse 27). This decree was not to *build* the house of the Lord, but to *beautify* it. The temple itself, of course, had already been built.

Ezra, chapter *Eight*, gives a list of those that went with Ezra to Jerusalem, and chapter *Nine* mentions how the Lord had given them "a reviving" and had allowed them "to set up the house of our God," giving them "a *wall* in Judah and in Jerusalem" (verse 9). Finally, Ezra, chapter *Ten*, tells us that people were called to Jerusalem from throughout Judea "and all the people sat in the *street* of the house of God" (verse 9). Mention of "the street" and the "wall" reminds us of the 70 weeks prophecy which said "the street shall be built again, and the wall, even in troublous times" (Daniel 9:25). Indeed those days were "troublous times."

We see, then, that *Cyrus*—according to Isaiah's prophecy—was to be the one that would speak the word which would cause Jerusalem to be rebuilt—both the city and temple. We believe this was a true prophecy. Josephus verifies it. The scriptural history we have seen also shows that the returning captives built not only the temple, but the city as well.

Notice the *timing*. The temple was completed in the sixth year of Darius (son of Hystaspes) (Ezra 6). It was after this—in the seventh year of Artaxerxes—that Ezra came to Jerusalem to beautify the house of God. And it was still later—in "the *twentieth* year of Artaxerxes the king" (Nehemiah 2:1) —that Nehemiah came to Jerusalem. After all these years, some in all seriousness tell us that only the temple had been built and that the commandment to rebuild the *city* was now given to *Nehemiah* by Artaxerxes! As one writer, representative of others, puts it: "The decree given to Nehemiah by Artaxerxes is the only one which has to do with rebuilding the *city;* therefore, it must be the same decree referred to by Gabriel as having to do with the beginning of the 70 weeks prophecy."[10]

But turning to the book of Nehemiah, we only have to read the first three chapters to see that by this time—after all these years since the return from Babylon—Jerusalem had *already* been rebuilt and there is nothing in the letters given to Nehemiah by Artaxerxes about the initial rebuilding of the city at all!

Nehemiah, chapter *One:* Certain ones came from Judah to see Nehemiah who served as the king's cup-bearer at Shushan. Nehemiah asked them concerning the Jews and Jerusalem. They reported that the Jews were in "great affliction and reproach" and that "the wall of Jerusalem" had been broken down and "the gates thereof" burned with fire. When Nehemiah heard these things, he "wept, and mourned certain days, and fasted, and prayed" (verses 1-4). Such reaction from Nehemiah clearly implies this was a report of comparatively *recent* damage to the walls and gates of Jerusalem—not what had happened clear back in the days of Nebuchadnezzar. *He had known about that all his life!*

Nehemiah, chapter *Two:* Nehemiah was so overcome with the news of what had happened at Jerusalem, he could not hide his sorrow—not even in the presence of the king. "Now I had not been beforetime sad in his presence. Wherefore the king said unto me, Why is thy countenance sad, seeing thou art not sick? This is nothing else but sorrow of heart." Nehemiah explained what had happened and asked permission to go unto Judah, to "the city of my fathers' sepulchers, that I may build it" (verse 5). (The word *build* here is of a broad meaning and, as we shall see, actually referred to the building or repairing of the parts that had been recently damaged—the walls and gates of the city—a work which was completed in 52 days!)

He was given "letters" from the king providing the nec-essary passport, as it were, to go into Judah and "a letter unto Asaph the keeper of the king's forest, that he may give me timber to make beams for the gates of the palace...and for the wall of the city, and for the house that I shall enter into" (verses 7,8). Nothing here could consti-tute the "decree" or "commandment" to restore and build Jerusalem mentioned in the seventy weeks prophecy.

Nehemiah, chapter *Three:* This chapter gives a list of those who built, that is, repaired the various parts of the wall. It is interesting to notice that the word "repaired" ap-pears 44 times in the Bible and 35 of these references are in this one chapter! We notice also several incidental refer-ences showing that houses had already been built before Nehemiah came to work on the walls. We read of "the

100

house of Eliashib, the high priest." Benjamin and Hashup repaired the wall "over against their house" and Azariah "by his house." There is mention of "the king's high house." The priests repaired "every one over against his house." Zadoc repaired "over against his house." Some had mortgaged their houses (Nehemiah 4:14; 5:3-13; 8:16).

Nehemiah hadn't come to Jerusalem to build houses —these had already been built years before. He came to work on the damaged *wall.* "Now it came to pass," said Nehemiah, "when...our enemies heard that I had builded the wall, and that there was no breach left therein; (though at that time I had not set up the doors upon the gates)...they thought to do me mischief" (Nehemiah 6:1,2). Nevertheless, "the wall was finished...IN FIFTY AND TWO DAYS. And it came to pass, that when all our enemies heard thereof...they perceived that this work was wrought of our God" (Nehemiah 6:15,16).

Due to threats from their enemies, Nehemiah gave regulations about opening and shutting the gates, and appointed "watches of the inhabitants of Jerusalem, every one in his watch, and every one to be over against *his house"* (Nehemiah 7:3). But the next verse says: "Now the city was large and great [margin, broad in spaces]; but the people were few, and the houses were not built" (verse 4). It is evident the people who lived there had houses. The meaning here, then, must be there were many vacant portions of land where houses had not been built yet.

But whether the city was ever completely rebuilt, or how long it may have taken to do so, has nothing to do with the starting point of the 70 weeks. These prophetic weeks were not to begin with the completion of the city, but from the going forth of the *commandment* to build Jerusalem. We believe the Biblical and historical evidence point to Cyrus as the one who issued this commandment. We would hasten to point out, however, that regardless of which decree is used, all Christians generally hold the belief in common that the 69 weeks (whether we understand perfectly the chronology or not) *did* indeed measure unto the Messiah—Jesus Christ. This, of course, is the main thing. With this background information in mind, we turn now to the text for the prophecy itself.

Seventy weeks are determined upon thy *people* and upon thy *holy city*, to finish the transgression, and to make an end of sins, and to make reconciliation for iniquity, and to bring in everlasting righteousness, and to seal up the vision and prophecy, and to anoint the most Holy.

Know therefore and *understand*, that from the going forth of the commandment to restore and to build Jerusalem unto the Messiah the Prince shall be seven weeks, and threescore and two weeks: the street shall be built again, and the wall, even in troublous times.

And *after* threescore and two weeks shall Messiah be cut off, but not for himself; and the people of the prince that shall come shall destroy the city and the sanctuary; and the end thereof shall be with a flood, and unto the end of the war desolations are determined.

And he shall confirm the covenant with many for one week: and in the midst of the week he shall cause the sacrifice and the oblation to cease, and for the overspreading of abominations he shall make it desolate, even until the consummation, and that determined shall be poured upon the desolate (Daniel 9:24-27).

Christians generally recognize that these seventy "weeks" or 490 days are symbolic of *years*—each day representing a year—that is, 490 years. Biblical examples of this measurement would include "a day for a year" mentioned by Ezekiel (Ezekiel 4:6) and the wandering of the Israelites in the wilderness for 40 years, a year for each day the spies were absent searching out the land (Numbers 14:34). It is also generally agreed that the "seven weeks, and threescore and two weeks," (that is, 69 weeks or 483 years), measured unto "Messiah." But concerning the final week of the prophecy, the seventieth week, two entirely different interpretations are held: the FUTURIST and the FULFILLED.

According to the futurist interpretation, a huge *gap* of 2,000 years or so separates the 70th week from the other 69 weeks that measured unto Messiah. The fulfilled interpretation does not require this gap, but holds that the 70th week followed the 69th in logical sequence. The futurist interpretation links the 70th week to the Antichrist

—that he will *make* a covenant with the Jews, allowing them to offer sacrifices in a rebuilt temple at Jerusalem, only to later *break* this covenant, causing sacrifices to cease. The fulfilled interpretation, links the 70th week to *Jesus Christ*—that he caused sacrifices to cease by becoming the perfect and final sacrifice at Calvary!

We believe the *fulfilled* interpretation regarding the 70th week is the correct position—that this is a prophecy about Jesus Christ, *not the Antichrist!* We will now notice, step by step, all of the basic parts of the 70 weeks prophecy and the fulfillment.

1. JERUSALEM WAS TO BE RESTORED. We have seen already the scriptures that explain this.

2. THE STREET AND WALL WERE TO BE REBUILT IN TROUBLOUS TIMES. We have seen in the book of Ezra some of the troubles that confronted the people in those years of rebuilding.

3. THE MOST HOLY WAS TO BE ANOINTED. We believe this refers to Jesus Christ. Gabriel announced to Mary: "The *holy* thing that shall be born of thee shall be called the Son of God" (Luke 1:35). Peter referred to him as "the *holy one*" (Acts 3:14). John referred to him as "the *holy one*" (1 John 2:20). Even demons had to recognize him as "the *holy one* of God" (Mark 1:24). David referred to him as "the *holy one*" who would not see corruption (Acts 2:27). Heavenly creatures rest not from saying: "*Holy, holy, holy*" concerning Christ (Revelation 4:8).

From the going forth of the commandment to restore and build Jerusalem unto Messiah was to be 483 years. When this time was fulfilled, those who know this prophecy were expecting the appearance of the Messiah, that is, *the Christ.* ("Christ" is the Greek form of the Hebrew word "Messiah.") Thus when John came baptizing, "the people were in *expectation,*" wondering if he were the Christ (Luke 3:15). John told them he was not the Christ—he was only the forerunner. When the time came that Jesus should be "made manifest to Israel" (John 1:29-31), he was baptized by John. "The heaven was opened. And the Holy Ghost descended in a bodily shape like a dove upon him, and a voice from heaven, which said, Thou art my beloved Son;

in thee I am well pleased" (Luke 3:21,22). Jesus had appeared to Israel right on time! The prophecy of Daniel had given the *time* for this, to which Jesus evidently referred in his statement: "The *time* is fulfilled" (Mark 1:15). Having now been introduced to Israel, having now been anointed with the Holy Spirit, as the Messiah (the Christ, the anointed one), he could announce in the Nazareth synagogue: "The Spirit of the Lord is upon me, because he hath *anointed* me" (Luke 4:18-22). He was the "holy" one that was "anointed" (Acts 4:27). "God *anointed* Jesus of Nazareth with the Holy Ghost...who went about doing good, healing all who were oppressed of the devil" (Acts 10:38).

4. MESSIAH WAS TO BE CUT OFF. The 69 weeks (7 plus 62) were to measure unto Messiah "and AFTER" the 69 weeks "shall Messiah be cut off." Now "after" 69 weeks cannot mean "in" or "during" the 69 weeks. If Messiah was to be cut off *after* the 69 weeks, there is only one prophetic week left in which he could have been cut off—the 70th week!—after three and a half years of ministry.

The term "cut off" implies that Messiah would not die a natural death; he would be murdered! So also had Isaiah prophesied using an equivalent word: "He was cut off out of the land of the living" (Isaiah 53:8). The details about how Messiah was "cut off" are given in the gospels.

5. "TO FINISH THE TRANSGRESSION," or literally, "to finish transgression." As Jesus was dying, he cried: "It is *finished.*" No future sacrifice can ever finish transgression; it was finished at Calvary (Hebrews 9:15). "He was wounded for our *transgressions*" (Isaiah 53:5).

6. "TO MAKE AN END OF SINS." Again we are pointed to Calvary. Jesus, who came "to save his people from their *sins,*" accomplished this when he *"put away sin* by the sacrifice of himself" (Matthew 1:21; Hebrews 9:26). Animal sacrifices could not "take away *sins*....But this man...offered one sacrifice for sins for ever" (Hebrews 10:4-17). The old sacrificial system could never make an end of sins, but Christ—by the sacrifice of himself—did make an end of sins, as the prophecy had said!

Jesus was "the Lamb of God," taking away "the sins of the world" (John 1:29). "Christ died for our sins" (1 Corinthians 15:3). He "bare our sins in his own body on the tree" (1 Peter 2:24). He "suffered for sins" (1 Peter 3:18). "He was manifested to take away our sins" (1 John 3:5). All of this does not mean, of course, there was no more sin in the world. What it does mean is this: At Calvary, the eternal sacrifice for sin was made, so that any and all—past, present, or future—who will be forgiven of sins will be forgiven because our Lord's death made an "end of sins"!

7. "TO MAKE RECONCILIATION FOR INIQUITY." The word reconciliation used here frequently appears in Leviticus as "to make atonement." Jesus, "our merciful and faithful high priest" made "reconciliation for the sins of the people" (Hebrews 2:17). "Having made peace through the blood...to reconcile all things unto himself...and you, that were sometimes alienated...hath he reconciled...through death" (Colossians 1:20-22; Ephesians 2:16). "God was in Christ, reconciling the world unto himself, not imputing their trespasses unto them; and hath committed unto us the word of reconciliation" (2 Corinthians 5:19). Plainly, "reconciliation for iniquity" was accomplished by Jesus, for he "gave himself for us, that he might redeem us from all iniquity" (Titus 2:14), and "the Lord hath laid on him the iniquity of us all" (Isaiah 53:6).

8. "TO BRING IN EVERLASTING RIGHTEOUSNESS." This too was accomplished by the redemptive work of Christ. "By the righteousness of one...shall many be made righteous" (Romans 5:17-21). He who came "to fulfill all righteousness" (Matthew 3:15) and who "loved righteousness and hated iniquity" (Hebrews 1:9), was made unto us "wisdom and righteousness" (1 Corinthians 1:30). "Who his own self bare our sins in his own body on the tree, that we, being dead to sins, should live unto righteousness" (1 Peter 2:24), "even the righteousness of God...through the redemption that is in Christ Jesus: whom God hath set forth to be a propitiation through faith in his blood to declare his righteousness for the remission of sins" (Romans 3:21-26). "For he hath made him to be sin for us...that we might be made the righteousness of God in him" (2 Corinthians 5:21).

Did Christ provide righteousness through his redemptive work? All Christians acknowledge that he did—and also that it was everlasting righteousness. "By his own blood he entered in once into the holy place, having obtained *eternal redemption*"—everlasting righteousness— "for us" (Hebrews 9:12). This everlasting righteousness is contrasted to the old sacrifices which were only of a *temporary* nature.

One only has to read the great redemption passages of Romans, Corinthians, Colossians, Ephesians, and Hebrews to see how an "end" of transgressions and sins, reconciliation for iniquity, and everlasting righteousness, were all accomplished by Christ at Calvary.

9. "TO SEAL UP VISION AND PROPHECY," or literally, "to seal up vision and prophet." The use of the metaphor "to seal" is derived from the ancient custom of attaching a seal to a document to show it was genuine (See 1 Kings 21:8; Jeremiah 32:10,11; cf. John 6:27). Christ "sealed" Old Testament prophecy by *fulfilling* what was written of him. "Those things which God before had showed by the mouth of all his prophets, that Christ should suffer he hath so *fulfilled*" (Acts 3:18). Of the Old Testament scriptures, Jesus said: "They are they which testify of me" (John 5:39). "All the prophets and the law prophesied until John" (Matthew 11:13), then John presented *Jesus* as he who was to be "made manifest to Israel." Jesus was the one that was to come—and we look for none other. *He* is the fulfillment of vision and prophecy.

10. "HE SHALL CONFIRM THE COVENANT." When Jesus instituted the Lord's supper, representative of his shed blood for the remission of sins, he said: "This is my blood of the new testament [covenant]" (Matthew 26:28). The word *testament* here and the word *covenant* are translated from exactly the same word. Through his shed blood, Christ "is the mediator of the new testament [covenant]" (Hebrews 9:14,15), "a minister...to *confirm* the promises made unto the fathers" (Romans 15:8).

Jesus is called the "mediator of the new *covenant*" (Hebrews 12:24), the "messenger of the *covenant*" (Malachi 3:1), and his blood is "the blood of the everlasting *covenant*" (Hebrews 13:20). Jesus Christ is the one who confirmed the covenant through his redemptive sacrifice at Calvary. How beautifully this harmonizes with what we have already seen!

106

11. "HE SHALL CAUSE THE SACRIFICE AND THE OB-LATION TO CEASE." The repeated sacrifices of the Old Testament were a mere type of the final sacrifice of Christ. Once he had made this sacrifice, "there remaineth no more sacrifice for sins" (Hebrews 10:18,16). After Calvary, for a few more years, the Jews continued *their* sacrifices, but these were not recognized by God. The death of Christ had provided the perfect and final sacrifice for sins.

Further proof that it was the death of Christ that caused sacrifice to cease, is seen in the *time element.* The prophecy said that sacrifice would cease in the *middle* of the week—after three and a half years—which was the length of Christ's ministry. As Eusebius, a Christian writer of the fourth century, wrote: "Now the whole period of our Savior's teaching and working of miracles is said to have been three and a half years, which is half a week. John the evangelist, in his Gospel makes this clear to the attentive."[11] Eusebius' mention of "half a week" clearly refers to Daniel's 70th week prophecy. His mention of the gospel of John refers to the four passovers during the ministry of Jesus (John 2:13, 5:1; 6:4, 13:1).*

After a ministry of three and a half years as the Christ—the anointed one—Jesus was cut off in death, in the middle of the 70th week of seven years. As Augustine said: "Daniel even defined the *time* when Christ was to come and suffer by the exact date."[12] Understanding this, we can now see real significance in certain New Testament statements. When some would have killed Jesus before this foreordained time, they could not, "because his *hour* was not yet come" (John 2:4, 7:30). On another occasion he said: "My *time* is not yet come" (John 7:6). Then just prior to his betrayal and death, he said, "My *time* is at hand," and finally, "the *hour* is come" (Matthew 26:18,45; John 17:1).

These and other verses clearly show there was a definite time in the divine plan when Jesus would die. He came to fulfill the scriptures, and there is only one Old Testament scripture which predicted the time of his

---

* John 5:1 does not mention the feast by name, but taking John 4:35 about the "four months" into consideration, it is possible to determine this was the feast of the passover.

death—the prophecy which stated that Messiah would be cut off in the midst of the 70th week—at the close of three and a half years of ministry. How perfectly the prophecy was fulfilled in Christ! But those who say the confirming of the covenant and causing sacrifices to cease in the midst of the week refers to a future Antichrist, completely destroy this beautiful fulfillment and are at a complete loss to show where in the Old Testament the *time* of our Lord's death was predicted.

The seventy weeks prophecy stated that Messiah would *confirm* the covenant (or would cause the covenant to *prevail*) with many of Daniel's people for the "week" or seven years. We ask then, When Christ came, was his ministry directed in a special way to Daniel's people—to *Israel* (Daniel 9:20)? Yes! John introduced him as he "that should be made manifest to *Israel*" (John 1:31). "I am not sent," Jesus said, "but unto the lost sheep of the house of *Israel*" (Matthew 15:24). And when he first sent out his apostles, they were directed: "Go not into the way of the Gentiles...go rather to the lost sheep of the house of *Israel*" (Matthew 10:5,6).

The first half of the "week," the time of our Lord's ministry, was definitely directed toward Israel. But what about the second half—the final three and a half years of the prophecy? Did the disciples continue to preach for the duration of the remaining three and a half years (as Christ's representatives) in some special way to Daniel's people—to Israel? Yes, they did.

Even though Jesus had told them the gospel was to go into all the world, to every creature (Mark 16:15), *yet* after the Ascension, for a period of time, the disciples still preached *only to Israel!* Why? We know of only one prophecy that would indicate this was to be the course followed: the prophecy of the 70 weeks. This may explain at least one reason why the gospel went "to the Jews *first*" and then later to the Gentiles (Romans 1:16). Peter preached shortly after Pentecost: "You are the children of the prophets, and of the *covenant*...unto you *first* God, having raised up his Son Jesus, sent him to bless you, in turning away every one of you from his iniquities" (Acts 3:25,26). Following the martyrdom of Stephen, Christians were scattered from Jerusalem and "went every where preaching the word," but still it was "to none but unto the Jews only" (Acts 8:4; 11:19). To the Jews Paul said, "It was *necessary* that the word of God should *first* have been spoken to you" (Acts 13:46).

In person, Christ came to Israel during the first half of the "week"—for three and a half years. *Through the disciples*—for the three and a half years that remained—his message still went to Israel, "the Lord *working with them*" (Mark 16:20). Then came the conversion of Cornelius which completely changed the missionary outreach, outlook, and ministry of the church (Acts 10). This marked, it would seem, the end of *exclusive* ministry to Israel, so that the gospel would now take its full mission to *all* people.

Numerous supernatural events that happened at this time clearly indicate this was a pivotal point in God's program. An angel appeared to Cornelius telling him to send for Peter. Through a vision of beasts and creeping things, Peter became aware that he was not to call any man common or unclean. At the house of Cornelius, while Peter was yet preaching, the Holy Spirit fell upon the Gentiles and they began to speak in tongues and magnify God.

Had three and a half years now passed since Christ was cut off in the midst of the week? After the day of Pentecost (which was 50 days after the crucifixion), we are not given exact dates for the events that led up to chapter 10. Some things happened quickly, like the conversion of three thousand in one day! Other things would have taken longer: selling possessions for the common treasury, the spread of rumors about certain widows being neglected, choosing seven deacons, and travel for ministry by Peter, John, Philip, and others. But all of these things could have easily fit within the space of three and a half years.

On the other hand, it does not seem that the time could have been a whole lot longer than this because of certain events that follow chapter 10. After staying "certain days" with Cornelius, Peter returned to Jerusalem. Barnabas traveled to Antioch where he preached for a time. After this he went to Tarsus to find Paul, who returned with him to Antioch, where for "a whole year" they taught much people. "In those days" a prophet named Agabus "signified by the Spirit that there should be great dearth throughout all the world: which came to pass *in the days of Claudius Caesar"* (Acts 11:22-28). Since Claudius did not come to power until 41 A.D., it is definitely implied that Agabus' prophecy was given prior to that year. Eventually relief was gathered for those in Judea and taken there by Paul and Barnabas (Acts 11:29,30). Then chapter 12 opens with the words: *"Now about that time* Herod the king stretched forth his hands to vex certain of the church..." This was Herod Agrippa I, who reigned from 37 A.D. until his death in 44 A.D. Thus the events of chapter 12 would have to fit within those dates. By chapter 15, during the council at Jerusalem, Peter mentioned how it had now been "a good while ago" that he had taken the gospel to the Gentiles at the house of Cornelius (Acts 15:7). We do not have *exact* dates here, but at least a general time frame as to that era of changeover when the outreach of the church began to include Gentiles.

12. THE DESTRUCTION OF JERUSALEM AND THE TEMPLE. This part of the prophecy was not dated within the framework of the 70 weeks as was the time of the appearance of Messiah to Israel, the time of his death, etc. Nevertheless, living on this side of the fulfillment, we know that the predicted destruction found fulfillment in 70 A.D. when the armies of Titus brought the city to desolation.

With the noted Biblical commentator, Adam Clarke, we say: "The *whole* of this prophecy from the times and corresponding events has been *fulfilled to the very letter."*[13]

THE FUTURIST INTERPRETATION CONSIDERED

Having presented what we believe to be the true interpretation of the 70th week prophecy, we will now examine the FUTURIST interpretation. In order for the 70th week to be future, those who hold this position insert a gigantic "gap" of about 2,000 years or so between the 69th and the 70th week. The confirming of the covenant for one "week" refers to a covenant the Antichrist will make with the Jews, a seven year agreement to allow them to offer sacrifices in a rebuilt temple at Jerusalem. But then, according to this view, in the middle of the week, he will break this covenant and cause sacrifices to cease.

But does the prophecy ever mention or refer to the Antichrist? According to the futurist interpretation, the Antichrist is referred to in Daniel 9:27. Well, let's see.

Verse 26: *Messiah* shall be cut off, but not for himself: and the *people* of the prince that shall come shall destroy the city and the sanctuary; and the end thereof shall be with a flood, and unto the end of the war desolations are determined.

Verse 27: And *he* shall confirm the covenant with many for one week; and in the midst of the week he shall cause the sacrifice and the oblation to cease.

We notice that verse 27 begins with the words: "And *he...*" To whom does the pronoun "he" refer? "He" could not refer to the Antichrist, for the Antichrist is *nowhere mentioned in the context!* The context does mention a "prince" whose *people* would destroy the city and the sanctuary. Since that destruction came in 70 A.D.—as both sides recognize—we see no reason to assume the "prince" is someone who will live 2,000 years later.

Regardless of this, we know that the pronoun "he" is not to be connected with the word "prince" in the expression "the people of the prince," for *prince* is the object of the modifying clause "of the prince." A pronoun *cannot* properly have as its antecedent the object of a modifying clause. To be grammatically correct, "he" must refer back to the word MESSIAH! The essence of the passage, then, is this: *"Messiah* shall be cut off...*he* shall confirm the covenant...*he* shall cause the sacrifice and oblation to cease."

But suppose we did connect "he" of verse 27 with the word "prince" in the phrase "the people of the prince that shall come shall destroy the city and the sanctuary." This would not indicate a future prince or Antichrist, for the people that destroyed Jerusalem were the Roman armies under the direction of Titus in 70 A.D. Those who hold the futurist viewpoint acknowledge that the "people" that destroyed Jerusalem were the Roman armies, but that the "prince" of those people *has not yet appeared!* Ironside says: "A prince is in view who is yet to play a large part in prophecy. He, however, *has not appeared yet,* but his people, that is, the Roman people, were used as a scourge of God to punish Israel for their sins, and they destroyed Jerusalem and the temple."[14] DeHaan says this prince "has not yet appeared,"[15] and Kelly: "That prince has *never yet come*....His people came and destroyed the city and the sanctuary; but he himself is not come."[16]

We have actually read dispensational books which quote the clause "the prince that SHALL come," as though the use of the word shall meant that the coming of this prince is *still* future! The coming of the prince was future in Daniel's time, of course, but so was the destruction of the city and sanctuary: "The people of the prince that *shall* come *shall* destroy the city and the sanctuary." How inconsistent to take a statement that was future *when written*, and now—over 2,000 years later—assume that the prophecy is still future on the basis of the word "shall"! There is not the slightest hint in this passage that the "people" were to come at one time, but their "prince" would not come until about 2,000 years after they had all died!

Nevertheless, those who hold the futurist view assume that "he" of Daniel 9:27 refers to a future prince, that this prince will be the Antichrist, and that he will make a covenant with the Jews—an agreement that will allow them to offer sacrifices in a rebuilt temple at Jerusalem! But as Guinness has well said: "Few would suppose that the notion has really *no solid ground at all in scripture*, but is derived from an erroneous interpretation of *one single clause of one single text!*"[17]

That single text is "Daniel 9:27." Daniel 9:27, Daniel 9:27, *Daniel 9:27*—over and over it is given as the reference for all kinds of theories about the Antichrist and his supposed treaty with the Jews! Notice the following examples:

"A treaty is proposed (Daniel 9:27)...the new Temple is set up, and once more the Jewish people follow the statutes of the Old Testament (Daniel 9:27)." But in the midst of the week, "the Antichrist proceeds at once to tear up the treaty, and to lay plans to shed every drop of Jewish blood."[18]

"He will make a treaty with the Jews, allowing them to...rebuild their temple, and begin anew their Old Testament sacrifices (Daniel 9:27)."[19]

"Antichrist will guarantee the Jews seven years of peace (Daniel 9:27)."[20]

"Antichrist makes a covenant with the mass of apostate Jews. Daniel 9:27. After three and a half years he breaks this covenant...and sets up in the Holy of Holies of the renewed temple, what is called...'the abomination of desolation.' Daniel 9:27."[21]

"According to Daniel 9:27, Antichrist will be here for seven years, for he makes a seven-year covenant with Israel, which will be the last seven years of this age."[22]

"'The Antichrist breaks his covenant with the Jewish people and causes the Jewish temple worship, according to the law of Moses, to cease (Daniel 9:27)."[23]

The fact is, Daniel 9:27 says *nothing* about a future rebuilt temple, *nothing* about restored sacrifices, *nothing* about the Antichrist making a covenant with the Jews! There are over 280 references to "covenant" in the scriptures and NOT ONE of them in any way introduces the idea of a covenant being made between the Jews and the Antichrist. Yet to hear some tell it, we might suppose this Antichrist covenant is as much a Biblical fact as God's covenant with Israel at Sinai!

"MAKE" A COVENANT?

Dispensational writers constantly use the word "MAKE" when speaking about this supposed covenant: "This covenant the Roman prince will *make* with the many" (Gaebelein); "Daniel's 'prince that shall come' ...*makes* a covenant with 'many'...permitting the restoration of the temple service" (Scofield). "When God takes up Israel again...a Roman prince will arise who will *make* a covenant with the nation for seven years" (Ironside). "The Bible tells us that the Antichrist shall *make* a covenant with Israel" (Roberts). "Antichrist will *make*...a covenant with Israel" (Dake). "Daniel's prediction also indicates that a prince...would *make* a firm covenant with the Jewish people" (Lindsey).

This whole idea that Antichrist will *make* a covenant with the Jews is supposedly taught in Daniel 9:27. But where does Daniel 9:27 say anything about the Antichrist—or anyone else for that matter!—"MAKING" a covenant? It is not there. The verse says the covenant

113

would be *confirmed,* or (as some translate it), the covenant would *prevail.* Daniel 9:27 says nothing about a covenant being *made.*

Nevertheless, once it is assumed that the Antichrist will *make* a covenant with the Jews, it is then taught that he will later *break* this covenant. Such wording is repeatedly used in dispensational writings.[24] It should be noticed, however, that neither term—*make* or *break*—appears in the text!

Daniel 9:27 says: "And he shall confirm the covenant with many for one week: and in the midst of the week he shall cause the sacrifice and oblation to cease." Once a person has the idea in mind that this verse is talking about the *Antichrist,* and that the Antichrist will *break* the covenant, it is then but another step to assume something else that destroys the true meaning altogether. Since sacrifices were to cease in the midst of the week, it is *assumed* that the covenant has to do with animal sacrifices in a rebuilt Jewish temple of the future! This is based on mere assumption.

The text says the covenant would be confirmed for a "week"—seven years. Then an event that would take place in the *middle* of the seven years is mentioned: sacrifice and oblation would cease. *There is no reason to assume that the second event is the undoing of the first.* To assume this actually makes the two statements contradictory. If the covenant is about allowing animal sacrifices, and if such sacrifices cease in the middle of the week, then it is evident the covenant would *not* prevail for seven years!

Briefly stated, the futurist position is that: (1) Daniel 9:27 refers to the *Antichrist,* (2) the Antichrist will *make* a covenant allowing the Jews to offer sacrifices, (3) he will *break* his covenant, and (4) the prophecy of the 70th week is *future.* The truth of the matter is: (1) Antichrist is *nowhere* mentioned in the passage, (2) *nothing* is said about a covenant being *made* to allow animal sacrifices, (3) *nothing* is said about a covenant being *broken,* and (4) the 70th week is not future, but has been *fulfilled!*

The covenant was to *prevail* with Daniel's people for the "week"—seven years—which it did through Christ. In the midst of the "week" Christ caused the sacrifice to cease in the divine program by himself becoming the perfect sacrifice for sins for ever!

Those who believe that the 70th week is yet future, however, argue that the covenant of Daniel 9:27 cannot refer to the covenant of Christ, for his covenant is an *"everlasting* covenant," whereas this covenant is only seven years in length.[25] But Daniel 9:27 does not say the covenant is seven years in length! What it does say is that the covenant would be confirmed or prevail with *Daniel's people* for the "week," that is, seven years. It is not a matter of how long the covenant itself would last, but how long the covenant would be confirmed *with Israel!*

Those who hold the futurist interpretation do not apply the expression "to anoint the most Holy" (Daniel 9:24) to Jesus Christ. They believe this refers to the anointing of a holy *place*—a future Jewish temple. It is pointed out that the term here translated "most Holy" appears 44 times in the Hebrew text and is usually used of things and places, not of persons. But as Hewitt has well said: "Even if 'most Holy' were never used of persons as such, it is doubtful if the Messianic interpretation would be seriously weakened. For Jesus called his body the 'temple' of God."[26] "Destroy this temple," Jesus said, "and in three days I will raise it up....He spake of his body" (John 2:19,21). We believe it was this "temple" that was anointed to bring about the purpose of God in the earth. The very title "Christ" means "the anointed one." We know also that the church, which is now the temple of God (Ephesians 2:20-22), was anointed with the Holy Spirit at Pentecost (Acts 2).

We see no reason for assuming "to anoint the most Holy" means the anointing of a future Jewish temple. Just why God would "anoint" a temple in which carnal sacrifices would be offered, in *direct conflict* with the finished work at Calvary, cannot be satisfactorily explained by those who hold the futurist interpretation.

The fact is, no future temple can be found in the prophecy of Daniel 9. At the time of Daniel, the Jerusalem temple had been destroyed. When they returned from the captivity, they rebuilt the temple. Then centuries later, according to the prophecy, people would come and "destroy the city and the sanctuary." This happened in 70 A.D.

Nothing is said about any other temple after this! Nevertheless, futurists must fit another temple, a future temple, an *unmentioned* temple, into their interpretation.

All together there are *six* things in Daniel 9:24 that were to be fulfilled in connection with the 70th week: to finish transgression, to make an end of sins, to make reconciliation for iniquity, to bring in everlasting righteousness, to seal up vision and prophecy, to anoint the most Holy. Those who hold the futurist position, as Dake, tell us: "The six events of verse 24 have *not been fulfilled.*"[27] H. A. Ironside has written:

> Israel did not recognize their Messiah. They do not know him yet as their sin bearer. Their transgression has not been finished. They do not know anything yet of atonement for iniquity. Everlasting righteousness has not been brought in. Vision and prophecy have not been sealed up. The most Holy has not been anointed by the return of the shekinah. What then?...Between the sixty-ninth and the seventieth weeks we have a *great parenthesis* which has now lasted over nineteen hundred years. The seventieth week has been *postponed* by God himself who changes the times and the seasons because of the transgression of the people....The moment Messiah died on the cross, *the prophetic clock stopped.* There has not been a tick upon that clock for nineteen centuries.[28]

According to this reasoning, the Jews did not recognize the Messiah, do not know him yet as their sin bearer, do not know anything of atonement, and so the 70th week had to be postponed. The fact is that "many" Israelites *did* receive Christ, *did* recognize him as their atonement and sin bearer. But regardless, the atonement *was* made at Calvary. It was a perfect and final work. In what possible sense, then, can these things be fulfilled in some future period of time?

Murray has well said:

> It is not without sorrow of heart that we listen to men, whose sincerity we do not question, emphasizing...that an end is not made of sin, that everlasting righteousness is yet to be brought in, and going so far as to attribute to a wicked Antichrist that which our glorious Lord has brought about by His sacrifice on the cross, the abolition of the oblation and sacrifice.[29]

Probably the most glaring discrepancy to the futurist interpretation of the 70th week is the way it requires a huge "gap" between the 69th and 70th week. With all due kindness to those who have taught and believed this, we feel that such a gap is unscriptural, unfounded, and contradictory. There are three basic periods contained within the seventy weeks prophecy. The first segment of seven "weeks" (49 years) was taken up with the work of rebuilding Jerusalem; the next segment of time, 62 "weeks" (434 years), was to reach unto Messiah; and the final period was one "week" (7 years). Even the strongest advocates of a gap between the 69th and 70th weeks, such as Kelly, say that "the first sixty-nine weeks ran *without a break*...uninterrupted."[30] If no gap is allowed between the 49 years and the 434 years, why should a gap of 2,000 years or more be placed between the 434 years and the 7 years?

The term "seventy weeks" is plural, but the Hebrew verb which is translated "determined" is *singular*. The actual wording (though it would be awkward to translate it this way into English) is: "Seventy weeks IS determined upon thy people and upon thy holy city." Barnes says: "In regard to the construction here—the singular verb with a plural noun....The true meaning seems to be, that the seventy weeks are spoken of collectively as denoting a period of time; that is, a period of seventy weeks is determined. The prophecy, in the use of the singular verb, seems to have contemplated the time, not as separate weeks, or as particular portions, but as *one* period."[31] The *Lange Commentary* says: "The verb being in the singular number indicates the *unity* or *singleness* of this entire period."[32]

The idea that an arbitrary gap can be placed in a time prophecy such as this, has been likened to a man with a yardstick who cut off the last inch and attached a piece of elastic between the 35th and 36th inches. Then he could stretch the 36th inch out as far as he wanted from the 35th inch. But in so doing, he defeated the very purpose for which the yardstick was intended! We believe the same inconsistency is involved in the futurist practice of separating the 70th week from the 69th week by a gap of 2,000 years or so.

Or the idea of a 2,000 year gap might be likened unto a man who plans a trip to Chicago. As he leaves Los Angeles, a sign tells him it is 70 miles!

After driving 69 miles, however, he is still in California, and Chicago is nowhere in view! A sign confirms that he has indeed come 69 miles from Los Angeles. It is now only one mile to Chicago—PLUS 2,000 MILES—*a parenthesis the first sign did not mention!*

The earliest record we have of anyone placing a gap between the 69th and 70th week is found in the third century in the writings of Hippolytus.[33] But this can add little weight to the present-day dispensational view, for he supposed the "weeks" measured from Cyrus to the *birth* of Christ. He figured the gap would then extend until about 500 A.D., the date he set for Christ's return. He believed the second coming would bring about the destruction of Antichrist, the resurrection of the dead, and the glorification of the saints.[34]

It was not until the rise of dispensationalism around 1830 and since, that the gap theory in its present form has spread—such being used in an attempt to support the secret rapture theory. We have actually heard well-meaning people argue that there will *have* to be a rapture of the church seven years before the end of the age, so Daniel's 70th week can be fulfilled!

Though often differing on *details*, especially in connection with the chronology involved, noted Christian leaders and reformers through the centuries have taught that the 70 weeks found complete fulfillment in connection with the *first* advent of Christ. Methodius connected the 70th week with Christ's first advent, as did Africanus who said: "...in the Savior's time...are transgressions abrogated, and sins brought to an end...everlasting righteousness is preached." Polychronius spoke of Christ confirming the covenant at the middle of the seventieth week.

Athanasius mentioned that the seventy weeks mark "both the actual date, and the divine sojourn of the Savior." He pointed out that some might "be able to find excuses to put off what is written to a future time. But what can they say to this...or can they face it at all? Where not only is the Christ referred to, but he...is declared to be not man simply, but Holy of Holies...." Eusebius placed the crucifixion in the midst of the 70th week and speaks of the covenant as the gospel. Augustine believed the 70th week found fulfillment in Christ's first coming and did not pertain to his second coming, for of that time no man knows the day or hour.

Bede, in his *The Explanation of the Apocalypse*, the earliest British exposition known, taught that the seventy

119

weeks pointed to Christ's first coming. John Wyclif said that "in the last week of years our Jesus confirmed those things which he promised the ancient fathers...when Christ preached and suffered." Heinrich Bullinger counted the seventy weeks as reaching unto the death of Christ. Luther linked the 70th week with the death of Christ and stated that during the 70th week the gospel was preached with power. Melanchthon figured that Jesus was crucified in the midst of the 70th week, three and a half years after his baptism. Calvin implied that the crucifixion occurred in the midst of the 70th week, when the sacrifice and offering ended.

Ephraim Huit, writer of the first systematic exposition on Daniel to appear in the American colonies, stated that "the last week finishes the sacrifice of the Lord, and begins both the calling of the Gentiles and the rejection of the Jews. Matthew Henry, of commentary fame, regarded the 70 weeks as referring to Christ's first coming, that during the final week the gospel was preached. Adam Clarke wrote that "the whole of this prophecy...has been fulfilled to the very letter."

Alexander Campbell summed it up well in these words: "In the middle of the week he [Christ] was to establish the New Institution...his ministry was three and a half years, or the middle of one week; then he was cut off. And in half a week, that is, three and a half years more, Christianity was sent to all nations. This *completes* the seventy weeks."

Briefly now, notice the contrast between the two interpretations we have discussed. The futurist position is that the 70th week is FUTURE; the fulfilled interpretation is that these things are now HISTORY. The futurist position is that ANTICHRIST will make a covenant with Israel; the fulfilled position is that CHRIST has already confirmed the covenant with Israel. The futurist position is that causing sacrifices to cease will be the work of the DEVIL; the fulfilled position is that causing sacrifices to cease was the work of GOD. The futurist interpretation requires a huge GAP; the fulfilled interpretation holds that the weeks followed each other in LOGICAL ORDER. The futurist position requires a yet future REBUILT TEMPLE; the fulfilled interpretation holds that the only temple mentioned in the prophecy was one that was to be DESTROYED.

We come now to a portion of the seventy weeks prophecy which has sometimes been neglected or completely overlooked. Many editions of the King James version include the following marginal rendering of Daniel 9:26: "...and [the Jews] they shall be no more his people, and the prince's [Messiah's] future people shall destroy the city and the sanctuary." This rendering, including the brackets, is given in the margin of Bibles published by such well known companies as Collins, Harper, Hertel, Holman, National, Nelson, Oxford, Whitman, Winston, World, and Zondervan. According to this, the people that were to destroy Jerusalem and the temple would be MESSIAH'S PEOPLE!

This interpretation is not based on the margin only; it can also be seen in the regular text. The prophecy spoke of the coming of "Messiah THE PRINCE." The next sentence says: "And the *people* of THE PRINCE that shall come shall destroy the city and the sanctuary"—wording that would normally indicate the prince in each sentence was the *same* person. If we were to say a certain prince is going to come, and then we make a statement about the *people* of the prince that shall come, none would take this to mean we are talking about a *good* prince in the first instance and a *wicked* prince in the second.

It is agreed that the prince in the first clause is Jesus Christ. We see no reason to believe the word prince in the clause that follows means the Antichrist. According to the margin, as well as the regular text, it appears that the subject all the way through the passage is *Messiah*. If correct, then it would be the people of Messiah the prince that would destroy the city and the sanctuary! More about this in a moment.

Something else we should notice is this: We have seen that "he" who was to confirm the covenant and "he" who would cause sacrifice to cease was Messiah. Then verse 27 goes on to say: "...*he* shall make it desolate." To be consistent, if "he" in the first part of verse 27 refers to Messiah, then so does it here. The subject is the desolation of Jerusalem (city and temple) and this passage indicates that Messiah would make it desolate.

121

But we all know and recognize that it was the *armies of Titus* that destroyed Jerusalem and the temple. How, then, are we to understand the statement that it would be the people of Messiah the prince that would destroy the city and the sanctuary (verse 26)? And, if Messiah is the subject of the passage, in what sense are we to understand that "he" would be the one to "make desolate" (verse 27)?

Since the prophecy spoke of Messiah bringing *blessings* upon Daniel's people and city, some have not understood that *he* would also be the one to bring *judgment.* But Messiah is both "Savior" and "Judge" (Luke 2:11; Acts 10:42). He is not only a "Lamb," but a "Lion" (Revelation 5:5,6); a "servant" and yet "King of kings" (Isaiah 53:11; 1 Timothy 6:15); a "man," and yet "the Lord from heaven" (1 Corinthians 15:47); the true foundation stone, and yet a stone of "stumbling" (1 Corinthians 3:11; 1 Peter 2:8).

Similar contrasts are seen in the Old Testament. If the people of the Lord were obedient, they would be "blessed" by him; if not, he would bring a "curse" upon them (Deuteronomy 28). He is a God not only of "compassion," but of "anger" (Micah 7:18,19; Hosea 6:1). "He was their *Savior.* In all their affliction he was afflicted, and the angel of his presence *saved* them: in his love and in his pity he *redeemed* them....But they rebelled, and vexed his holy Spirit; therefore he was turned to be their *enemy*, and he fought against them" (Isaiah 63:8-10).

Now if the Savior and Redeemer in the *Old* Testament was "turned" and became the "enemy" of, and "fought against" that rebellious people, it is not inconsistent to believe that he who is revealed as the Savior and Redeemer of the *New* Testament could also bring judgment upon those who rebelled against him and rejected his holy Spirit. There is no straining of argument here, but patience is required to study it all out.

Since Christ will be the one that will judge the world in the appointed day of judgment (Acts 17:31), why should we suppose that he who was given "all power in heaven and in earth" (Matthew 28:18), could not bring judgment upon a reprobate city in 70 A.D.?

All Christians acknowledge that the judgment that fell upon Jerusalem was the judgment of God, that is *divine* judgment. But many have not thought of this judgment as being the work of the *son* of God, the Messiah. However, it is clearly stated: "The Father...hath committed *all* judgment unto the Son...and hath given him authority to *execute* judgment" (John 5:22,26,27).

It may sound strange to speak of the destruction of Jerusalem as being accomplished by the *Lord*, knowing it was the armies of Titus that did the work of destruction. But we are on solid Bible ground. Repeatedly, the Lord said, "*I* will do this..." and yet the context shows that heathen armies were his instruments:

> "Thus saith the Lord...*I* will...take Nebuchadnezzar the king of Babylon, *my servant*...he shall smite the land of Egypt...and *I* will kindle a fire in the house of the gods of Egypt...and the houses of the gods of the Egyptians shall he burn with fire" (Jeremiah 43:10-13). "*I* will also make the multitude of Egypt cease...*by the hand of Nebuchadezzar* king of Babylon. He and his people with him shall...destroy the land...thus will *I* execute judgments in Egypt" (Ezekiel 30:10-19). "*By the sword of the mighty* will *I* cause thy multitude to fall...*I* shall make the land of Egypt desolate" (Ezekiel 32:9-15). "*I* will bring upon Tyrus Nebuchadnezzar king of Babylon...with horses and chariots....He shall slay with the sword...he shall set engines of war against thy walls" (Ezekiel 26:7). "*I* will send a fire on the wall of Tyrus" (Amos 1:10).

These verses and many, many more,[35] speak of the *Lord* bringing various judgments, even though human armies were his instruments. The same wording was used to describe judgments that Jerusalem and Judah faced in the Old Testament:

> "The *Lord* shall bring a nation against thee from far" (Deuteronomy 28:49). "My soul shall abhor you and *I* will make your cities waste, and bring the land into desolation" (Leviticus 26:30-33). "*I* will bring evil upon this people...a people cometh from the north country...they shall lay hold on bow and spear; they are cruel, and have no mercy...they ride upon horses, set in array as men for war against thee, O daughter of Zion" (Jeremiah 6:18-23). "*I* will give this city [Jerusalem] into the hand of the king of Babylon...*I* will command, saith the Lord...and they shall fight against it, and take it, and burn it with fire: and *I* will make the cities of Judah a desolation" (Jeremiah 34:2,22). "*I* will send a fire upon

Judah, and it shall devour the palaces of Jerusalem" (Amos 2:5). "I will dash them one against another...I will not pity...but destroy them....Woe unto thee, O Jerusalem!" (Jeremiah 13:9-27). "I will make...this city a curse to all nations...desolate" (Jeremiah 26:1-9). "I will even make the pile for the fire great...I will profane my sanctuary" (Ezekiel 24:9,21). "Shall there be evil in a city, and the Lord hath not done it?...Therefore will I deliver up the city with all that is therein" (Amos 2:5; 6:8). "I am against thee, and will execute judgments" (Ezekiel 5:8-17). "I will send...Nebuchadnezzar the king of Babylon, my servant...against this land...and will utterly destroy" (Jeremiah 25:8-11).

These, and many more scriptures,[36] show that the destruction that came upon Judah and Jerusalem was carried out by human armies. Because they were carrying out the judgment of God, the Lord spoke of them as *his people*, their work as *his work*, and their leader as *his servant!*

Now if such wording is understood in the destruction that came upon Jerusalem in the Old Testament, this same wording cannot be out of place when describing what happened to the same city in 70 A.D. At that time, Roman armies destroyed Jerusalem—a fact of history. But since this was the *Lord's* judgment, we could also correctly say that Jerusalem was destroyed by the *Lord*. Thus "the people of the prince [Messiah, the Lord]" destroyed the city and the sanctuary. They were not his people in the sense they were Christians, but in the sense they carried out his judgment, even as Nebuchadnezzar's armies had been his people in the destruction of Jerusalem at an earlier time.

Messiah the Prince is the subject all the way through the passage. Once we understand this, it no longer matters whether the word "he" of verse 27 is connected with the word "prince" in the phrase "the people of the prince," or with "Messiah the prince," for in a definite sense *both* expressions refer to Messiah!

Looking again at the prophecy, we read: "And the people of the prince [Messiah] that shall come shall destroy the city and the sanctuary; and the end thereof [the destruction of the city and sanctuary] shall be with a *flood*" (Daniel 9:26). "Flood" here is from a root word, commonly translated *overflow* (Strong's Concordance, 7857,

7858). It is repeatedly used in Daniel in the sense of the overflowing of an enemy invasion (Daniel 11:10,22,26,40).

It is not unusual for the scriptures to use the word flood in this way. "The *floods* of ungodly men made me afraid" (Psalms 18:4). "The enemy shall come in like a *flood*" (Isaiah 59:19). "Who is this that cometh up as a *flood?*...he saith, I will go up...I will destroy...rage ye chariots and let the mighty men come forth" (Jeremiah 46:7-9). Invading armies are likened to "an overflowing *flood*" (Jeremiah 47:2,3) and "an overrunning *flood*" (Nahum 1:8).

According to Daniel's prophecy, the "end" that was to come upon Jerusalem and the temple would be "with a flood"—the flood of an invading enemy army, a fact confirmed by the historic fulfillment. As the Romans hammered away at the massive gates and city walls, at various places breaches were made and a rush of warriors from the far away Tiber flowed into the city like an overwhelming flood, bringing it to destruction.[6]

The prophecy continues with these words: "And unto the end of the war [against Jerusalem] desolations are determined," or as the margin says: "It shall be cut off by desolations." This work of destruction is further described in verse 27: "And for the overspreading of *abominations* he [Messiah, the Lord] shall make it desolate." According to Jesus' own interpretation, the abomination that would make desolate would be Gentile armies (Matthew 24:15; Luke 21:20). Bearing this in mind, notice this verse again: "And for"—on behalf of—"the overspreading of abominations [the invading Gentile armies] he [Messiah, the Lord] shall make it desolate." God would move "for" these heathen armies spreading around Jerusalem to take it. Or as the margin has it: "With the abominable *armies*, he shall make it desolate." These armies were but his instruments to carry out his judgment.

To what extent did the prophecy say these heathen armies would cause desolation in Jerusalem? Would they merely destroy a small portion of a wall, or maybe just a portion of the temple, or a few houses? No, the prophecy continues by saying the Lord with abominable armies would "make it desolate, even until the consummation"—the complete destruction. As Jesus had said when commenting on this very prophecy: "One stone shall not be left upon another that shall not be thrown down!" (Matthew 24:2).

The Jewish nation had filled the cup of iniquity full. They had rejected and killed the Messiah and persecuted those he sent unto them. What Jesus said in the parable of the marriage feast perfectly fits the divine judgment that fell upon Jerusalem. They rejected the king's invitation and killed his messengers. Consequently, "when the king heard thereof, he was wroth: and sent forth *his armies* and destroyed those murderers, and burned up their *city"* (Matthew 22:7).

The prophecy of Daniel 9 said that 69 weeks would measure unto Messiah, which they did. After this, he was cut off in the midst of the remaining week—the 70th week —becoming the perfect and final sacrifice in God's plan. Through his redemptive work, he made an end of sins, made reconciliation for iniquity, and brought in everlasting righteousness through the gospel. The grand theme of the prophecy is *Jesus Christ!* Its great fulfillment shines forth from Calvary with glory and power! Its timing is perfect. Its words harmonious. Its message satisfies the soul. To cast all of this aside and attempt to apply much of the prophecy to a time yet future and to the *Antichrist* (instead of Christ and his redemptive work at Calvary) is, we feel, a serious error. We appeal to all brethren who have taught or believed this to reconsider this interpretation in the light of the Scriptures.

*   *   *   *   *   *   *   *   *   *   *

In our study of the 70 weeks, we have seen that Antichrist is nowhere mentioned or referred to in Daniel 9, nothing is said about him making and breaking a covenant with the Jews, etc. What, then, do the scriptures teach concerning Antichrist? What did Paul mean when he said the man of sin would exalt himself above all others in the "temple of God"? Did he mean a rebuilt Jewish temple? Since Paul said that Christ will not come again until there is a falling away first and the man of sin is revealed, we ask: Has the falling away occurred yet? Has the man of sin been revealed? Is his appearance future or fulfilled? These are the things to be considered in the section that follows.

Part Four:

THE ANTICHRIST

Futurist and Fulfilled Views Compared

The "Antichrist" gets a lot of publicity these days—on religious radio and television programs, in prophetic novels which are sensational and scary, and even in motion pictures. The common conception is that he will be an atheistic politician who will appear in the near future with vast control of jet planes, rockets, bombs, computers, spy systems, and cause all manner of hell to break out on planet earth.

During World War I, some believed the Kaiser would be the dreaded man of sin, the Antichrist. A few years later it was Joseph Stalin. When the New Deal came into power in the United States, some thought Franklin Roosevelt was at least the forerunner of Antichrist. Others believed Hitler or Mussolini were likely candidates. A book published in 1940 asked the question: "Is Mussolini the Antichrist?" and the writer answered: "He may be. I know of no reason why he should not fit the description of this terrible man of sin....He is evidently an atheist."[1] Another writer claimed that Mussolini had fulfilled forty-nine of the prophecies concerning Antichrist!

127

Others have thought the Antichrist will be Nimrod, Nero, or a Roman Emperor resurrected from the dead. Some believe it will be Judas Iscariot. After comparing John 17:12 with 2 Thessalonians 2:3, one writer says: "Judas, then, will be the Antichrist."[2] Another put it this way: "Antichrist will be Judas come to earth again!"[3]

Some believe the Antichrist will be assassinated and that Satan will raise him from the dead. A well known preacher writes: "The Bible tells how, right in the middle of his rise to power, Antichrist will be assassinated. The devil will then make his big move. He will raise Antichrist from the dead in an attempt to reproduce the Holy Trinity."[4] Though often differing on details, futurists all believe the Antichrist is someone yet to appear on the world scene and, with each passing year, promote this leader or that as the most likely candidate.

In contrast to the futurist position is what we will call the FULFILLED interpretation—that the prophecies concerning the man of sin or Antichrist have found their fulfillment in the *Papacy*—the succession of popes that rose to power in Rome following the fall of the Roman Empire. To some, this interpretation will appear too *ridiculous* to even consider, and it will be cast aside immediately. But before such actions are taken, surely the evidence for this position should be carefully examined. Right or wrong, such noted men as Wyclif, Huss, Luther, Calvin, Knox, Zwingli, Tyndale, Foxe, Newton, and Wesley, all believed that the prophecies of the man of sin had found their fulfillment in the Roman Papacy. Should we not at least inquire *why* these men believed this way? When all the evidence is in, we do not believe the fulfilled interpretation will appear as absurd as some have thought.

"HE WHO LETTETH WILL LET"

When the Christians at Thessalonica supposed the day of the Lord's coming was right at hand, Paul explained there were certain events that would happen before that time. There would come "a falling away first, and that *man of sin* be revealed." And before the man of sin could be revealed, something else would need to happen. There was something restraining, holding back his appearance— something that would need to be taken out of the way:

Remember not, that, when I was yet with you, I told you these things? And now you know *what* withholdeth that he [the man of sin] might be revealed in his time. For the mystery of iniquity doth already work: only he who now *letteth* [restrains] will *let* [restrain], until *he* be taken out of the way. And then shall that Wicked be revealed (2 Thessalonians 2:1-8).

Though Paul does not call this "let" or restraint by name, his words show it was not something unknown or obscure. He *knew* what it was. The Christians at Thessalonica *knew* what it was. Solid evidence shows that the Christians of the early centuries believed it was the ROMAN EMPIRE that was in the way, the fall of which would bring on the man of sin. When they were accused of holding this belief, they did not deny it. Their reply was that they did not wish the fall of the Empire, for its fall would bring on the Antichrist. As Lactantius phrased it: "Beseech the God of heaven that the Roman State might be preserved, lest, more speedily than we suppose, that hateful tyrant should come."[5]

Justin Martyr spoke of Christians praying for the continuance of the restraining Roman Empire, lest the dreaded times of Antichrist, expected to follow upon its fall, should overtake them in their day.[6] Hippolytus believed the breaking up of the fourth Empire, Rome, would bring on the Antichrist who would persecute the saints.[7] Tertullian said: "What is the restraining power? What but the Roman State, the breaking up of which, by being scattered into ten kingdoms, shall introduce Antichrist upon [its own ruins]?"[8]

Cyril of Jerusalem, in the fourth century, speaking of this same prophecy said: "This, the predicted Antichrist, will come, when the times of the Roman Empire shall be fulfilled....Ten kings of the Romans shall arise together...among these the eleventh is Antichrist, who, by magical and wicked artifices, shall seize the Roman power."[9]

Jerome, noted bishop and translator, stated: "He [Paul] shows that that which restrains is the Roman Empire; for unless it shall have been destroyed, and taken out of the midst, according to the prophet Daniel, Antichrist will not come before that."[10] "Let us therefore say what *all* ecclesiastical writers have delivered to us, that when the Roman Empire is destroyed, ten kings will divide the Roman world among themselves, and then will be revealed the man of sin."[11]

Ambrose said the Roman Empire was that which was holding back the appearance of Antichrist and that "after the failing or decay of the Roman Empire, Antichrist would appear."[12] Chrysostom stated: "One may naturally enquire, What is that which withholdeth?" He answered that it was the Roman Empire and that "when the Roman Empire is taken out of the way, then he [Antichrist] shall come. And naturally. For as long as the fear of this empire lasts, no one will willingly exalt himself, but when that is dissolved, he will attack the anarchy, and endeavor to seize upon the government both of man and of God."[13]

"We have the consenting testimony of the early fathers," says Elliott, "from Irenaeus (130-200 A.D.), the disciple of the disciple of St. John, down to Chrysostom (347-404) and Jerome (331-420) to the effect that it was understood to be the Imperial power ruling and residing at Rome."[14] The *Expositor's Bible Commentary* says: "There is no reason to doubt that those fathers of the church are right who identified it with the Empire of Rome and its sovereign head."[15] After many pages of carefully documented proof for his statement, Froom says that the "letting" or restraining power impeding the development of the "man of sin" was interpreted in the early church as the Roman Empire.[16]

Guinness says: "The early writings of the fathers tell us with remarkable unanimity that this 'let' or hindrance was the Roman Empire as governed by the Caesar; and that on the fall of the Caesar, he [the man of sin] would arise."[17] *Clarke's Commentary* states that the *united* testimony of the church leaders of those first centuries was that the restraint which was to be removed was the Roman Empire.[18] The *Encyclopedia Britannica* says this was *universally* believed by Christians.[19]

Now we can understand why Paul was careful, when writing about it, not to mention the restraint by name. To teach that "eternal Rome" would fall could have brought on unnecessary conflict with the leaders of the Empire within which they lived. Especially when writing to the Christians at Thessalonica would this caution be in order, for it was there they had been accused of doing things "contrary to the decrees of Caesar" and believing in "another king, one Jesus" (Acts 17:7). Wisdom had it that he would simply write: "Remember...when I was yet with you, I told you these things?" (2 Thessalonians 2:5).

Jerome understood why Paul was careful in this matter: "If he had chosen to say this *openly*, he would have foolishly aroused a frenzy of persecution against the Christians,"[20] and Chrysostom stated: "Because he said this of the Roman Empire, he naturally glanced at it, and speaks covertly and darkly. For he did not wish to bring upon himself superfluous enmities, and useless dangers."[21]

Understanding that it was the Roman Empire that would fall, the fall of which would bring on the man of sin, we now have a TIME frame for the prophecy! Since the fall of Rome is now long past, it is strongly inferred that we should look for the rise of the man of sin in a *historical* context—not the future. But more about this in a moment.

Looking again at Paul's prophecy (2 Thessalonians 2:6,7), he mentions that something ("what") was restraining—and also someone ("he"). "What" is neuter gender; "he" is masculine. Paul evidently referred to the *Roman Empire* as "what," and the *Caesar* as "he." If, then, the Caesar would have to be "taken out of the way" for the man of sin to come to power, we have a strong indication of WHERE the man of sin would rule.

To illustrate, suppose we wanted to build a house on a certain piece of property, but another building was in the way. Obviously it could not be said that the old building was *in the way*—and needed to be taken *out of the way*—unless it was occupying the spot where the new house would be built! Understood in the context of the prophecy before us, the man of sin would rise to power in the same place that the Caesar ruled: *Rome!* The man of sin would be a Roman power!

Thus we know WHERE he would rise to power and we know WHEN! Looking into history, what power rose up in Rome following the fall of the Empire? We believe the evidence all points to the PAPACY. The highly esteemed Bibli-

131

cal commentator, Albert Barnes, has well said: "To any acquainted with the decline and fall of the Roman Empire, nothing can be more manifest than the correspondence of the facts in history respecting the rise of the Papacy, and the statement of the apostle Paul here."[22]

The breaking up of the Roman Empire and the removal of the Caesar from power in Rome took place over a period of time. Says the historian Flick: "The removal of the capital of the Empire from Rome to Constantinople in 330, left the Western Church practically free from Imperial power, to develop its own form of organization. The Bishop of Rome, *in the seat of the Caesars*, was now the greatest man in the West and was soon forced to become political as well as spiritual head."[23] Cardinal Manning wrote: "The possession of the pontiffs, commences with the abandonment of Rome by the emperors."[24]

Finally in 476, the last Western Caesar, Augustulus, was forced out of office by the Goths. With the fulfillment of these things, the mighty Roman Empire of the Caesars had passed from the scene of human history. The restraint was now fully *ek mesou*, "out of the way." According to what Paul had written, the stage had now been cleared for the next scene in the prophetic drama: the rise to power of the man of sin. Guiness has written:

> The mighty Caesars had fallen; Augustus, Domitian, Hadrian, Diocletian, were gone; even the Constantines and Julians had passed away. The seat of sovereignty had been removed from Rome to Constantinople. Goths and Vandals had overthrown the western empire; the once mighty political structure lay shivered into broken fragments. The imperial government was slain by the Gothic sword. The Caesars were no more, and Rome was an actual desolation. Then slowly on the ruins of old imperial Rome rose another power and another monarchy—a monarchy of loftier aspirations and more resistless might, claiming dominion, not alone over the bodies, but over the consciences and souls of men; dominion, not only within the limits of the fallen empire, but throughout the entire world. Higher and higher rose the Papacy, till in the Dark Ages all Christendom was subjected to its sway."[25]

Once it is admitted that the Roman Empire under the rule of the Caesar was that which was holding back the

132

appearance of the man of sin, it is evident that the Papacy —rising to power at the time and place indicated—met the requirements of the prophecy. How, then, is this countered by those who hold the futurist position? Usually all evidence about the Roman Empire being the restraint is *ignored* and statements, such as the following, are made:

"The hindering influence in this passage is, of course, the ministry of the Holy Spirit in and through the lives of Christians today."[26] "This One who hinders the man of sin must be the Holy Spirit. At the rapture of the saints, we believe, the Holy Spirit will be taken out of the way of the man of sin so that he may be revealed."[27] Such writers merely echo the theory spread by Scofield that the restrainer "can be no other than the Holy Spirit in the Church, to be 'taken out of the way'."[28] But as Oswald Smith has well said concerning the verse under consideration: "There is *no mention of the Holy Spirit at all*. That is a Scofield Bible assumption. The Holy Spirit and the church remain to the *end* of the age."[29]

HOLY SPIRIT? CHURCH?

As Christians, we all recognize, of course, that the Holy Spirit within the church is a great force against evil. But this was not the restraint of which Paul spoke. He told the Thessalonians that the coming of the Lord to gather the church would NOT take place until *after* the man of sin would be revealed (2 Thessalonians 2:1-3). To then turn right around and say the church would be taken out of the way *before* the man of sin would be revealed, would be a direct contradiction!

We have seen the reason why Paul was careful not to mention the restraint by name when writing to the Thessalonians. But if the restraint had been the Holy Spirit or the church, there would be no reason for this caution. Indeed, several times in his writings to the Christians at Thessalonica, he mentioned the church and the Holy Spirit (1 Thessalonians 1:1,5,6; 2:14; 4:8; 5:19; etc.).

There is no record of anyone believing that the restraint mentioned by Paul was the Spirit until the latter half of the *fourth* century and we only know of this belief because Chrysostom *rejected it.* He wrote: "Some indeed say, the grace of the Spirit." But he points out that the restraint was the Roman Empire and could not be the Spirit. "Wherefore? Because if he [Paul] meant to say the Spirit, he would not have spoken obscurely, but *plainly.*"

What Chrysostom rejected was a theory about the restraint being the grace of the Spirit in connection with *spiritual gifts.* It had nothing to do with the dispensational idea of the Spirit being taken out of the world in a secret rapture of the church. The teaching that the Holy Spirit will be taken out "seems to be of quite *modern* origin; there is, apparently, *no trace* of it in early writings on the subject."[30]

UNPARALLELED WORLD EVANGELISM?

Those who hold this belief face serious problems of interpretation. They teach that after the church is gone, God will turn to the Jews, a believing remnant of which will preach the gospel of the kingdom into all the world. They will be *so empowered,* some ask us to believe, they "will become the mightiest evangelists this world has ever seen."[31]

According to a popular dispensational book, *The Late Great Planet Earth,* "They are going to be 144,000 Jewish Billy Grahams turned loose on this earth—the earth will never know a period of evangelism like this period....They are going to have *the greatest number of converts in all history*"[32]

But how, we ask, will these Jews be so empowered if the Holy Spirit, who convicts and converts, is taken from the earth? We have carefully checked the arguments that are given to explain this glaring discrepancy. To us, they are weak and unconvincing.

There is no reason to believe that the restraint of which Paul wrote was the Holy Spirit or the church. We have solid evidence that the early Christians believed it was the Roman Empire, that it would be taken out of the way, and then the man of sin would be revealed. We know it was Paul's practice to prove what he taught from the scriptures. In this case, his teaching about the fall of the Roman Empire, was apparently based on Daniel Seven, to which we now turn.

In vision, Daniel saw four great beasts which symbolized four kingdoms which were to rule the earth (Daniel 7).

1. The first beast was like a lion with eagle's wings, but the wings were to be plucked off (Daniel 7:4). Even as the lion among animals is the king of the forest, so the empire which held first position in the vision was *Babylon.* In due time, its "wings" were plucked off and mighty Babylon fell from its exalted position.

2. The second beast was like a bear and it had three ribs in its mouth (Daniel 7:5). Even as a bear is less courageous (as well as less noble) than the lion, the second kingdom, *Medo-Persia,* was less in glory. It fell short of Babylon in wealth, magnificence, and brilliance. The mention of "three ribs" in the mouth—between the teeth where a bear crushes its prey—is possibly a reference to the fact that Medo-Persia crushed the three provinces that made up the Babylonian kingdom: Babylon, Lydia, and Egypt.

3. The third beast was like a leopard with four wings and four heads (Daniel 7:6). The third kingdom, the *Grecian Empire* of Alexander the Great, was symbolized by the leopard which is noted for its quick movements and remarkable swiftness by which it springs upon its prey. Likewise, the conquests of Alexander were amazingly rapid. At the age of 32, it is said, he had conquered the world and wept because there were no more worlds to conquer.

The four heads on this leopard beast probably symbolized the four kings who ruled after the death of Alexander: (1) Cassander ruled over Greece and the surrounding country, (2) Lysimachus ruled over Asia Minor, (3) Selecus ruled over Syria and Babylon, and (4) Ptolemy ruled over Egypt.

4. The fourth beast that Daniel saw was "dreadful and terrible, and strong exceedingly; and it had great iron teeth: it devoured and brake in pieces, and stamped the residue with the feet of it, and it was diverse from all the beasts that were before it; and it had ten horns" (Daniel 7:7). The fourth world kingdom was the *Roman Empire.* As the prophecy said, it was dreadful, terrible, and strong; it

135

did tear down the whole earth; and it stands out as diverse from the other empires of history. The meaning of the ten horns on this beast is explained in verse 24: "These ten horns out of this kingdom are ten kings [or kingdoms]* that shall arise." Macchiavelli, the Roman historian, described the Empire as being divided among the various Gothic tribes—their number being *ten:* Heruli, Suevi, Burgundians, Huns, Ostrogoths, Visigoths, Vandals, Lombards, Franks, and Anglo-Saxons. These have ever since been spoken of as the ten kingdoms that rose out of the Roman Empire.

"I considered the horns," Daniel continues, "and, behold, there came up among them another *little horn,* before whom there were three of the first horns plucked up by the roots: and, behold, in this horn were *eyes* like the eyes of a man, and a *mouth* speaking great things" (verse 8). This "little horn" would make *war against the saints* (verse 21) and would think to *change times and laws* (verse 25). Altogether there are eight things that we should notice concerning the little horn.

1. The little horn was to be a ROMAN power. A horn on a beast is that which grows out of a beast. Since we know the fourth beast was Roman, so also must the horn be *Roman!* Does the Papacy fit this description? Yes. The Papacy rose to power at the time and place indicated by Bible prophecy. No one can question that the Papacy is Roman. Its seat is in Rome. Its very name is *Roman* Catholic, an amazing point of identification even in our time!

2. The little horn was to be revealed in power among the ten kingdoms into which the Roman Empire was divided. We have seen that Rome was divided into ten kingdoms. The Papacy *did* rise to power among these ten kingdoms—following the fall of Rome.

3. The little horn was to pluck up three of the other horns, the interpretation being that "he shall subdue three kings [kingdoms]" (Daniel 7:24). Did the Papacy subdue three of these ten kingdoms? Eliott says: "I might cite

---

* In Daniel 7 the words "kings" and "kingdoms" are used interchangeably. The prophecy speaks of four kings (verse 17) and goes on to speak of these as four *kingdoms* (verse 23). There is no contradiction here—if there is a king, there is of necessity a kingdom.

three that were eradicated from before the Pope out of the list first given, viz., the Heruli under Odacer, the Vandals, and the Ostrogoths."[33] The Heruli were overthrown in 493, the Vandals in 534, and the Ostrogoths in 553.

4. The little horn would rise up among the ten horns (kingdoms), but would be "diverse." Has the Papacy been a kingdom that has been different from other kingdoms that rose up out of the fourth beast? Yes. Other kingdoms have claimed temporal power, but the Papacy claimed spiritual power as well. The Papacy is the only government rising from the ruins of Rome that made such claims. It has claimed its diversity is as the sun compared to the moon. Guinness has put it well:

> Is not the Papacy sufficiently diverse from all the rest of the kingdoms of western Europe to identify it as the little horn? What other ruling monarch of Christendom ever pretended to apostolic authority, or ruled men in the name of God? Does the Pope dress in royal robes? Nay, but in priestly garments. Does he wear a crown? Nay, but a triple tiara, to show that he reigns in heaven, earth, and hell! Does he wield a scepter? Nay, but a crosier or crook, to show that he is the good shepherd of the Church. Do his subjects kiss his hand? Nay, but his toe! Verily this power is 'diverse' from the rest, both in great things and little. It is small in size, gigantic in its pretensions.[34]

5. The little horn was pictured with a MOUTH—"a mouth that spoke very great things" and "great words against the most High" (Daniel 7:20,25). This suggests pride and arrogance. By teaching corrupt doctrines, the Papacy has spoken against God. It should be carefully noted that the prophecy tells what this little horn would *do*, not what he would *profess to do*. He professes to speak the words of God, to define the doctrines of God; but in reality, he speaks things that are unscriptural and, in some cases, even opposite to scripture.

Among many great claims the popes have made, especially arrogant is the *Unam Sanctam* of Boniface VIII: "All the faithful of Christ by necessity of salvation are subject to the Roman pontiff, who judges all men....Therefore we declare, assert, define, and pronounce, that to be subject to the Roman pontiff is to every human creature altogether *necessary for salvation*"! The Papacy has had a mouth claiming things that no bishop had ever claimed before. The sentences of the Pope are considered final; his utterances infallible; his decrees irreformable.

6. The little horn of Daniel's vision "had eyes" and his "look was more stout than his fellows" (Daniel 7:20). Because a horn on a beast does not normally possess eyes, such symbolism stands out vividly. This horn would be a power with foresight, intelligence. With such eyes, it would be a seer. Does the Papacy fit this? The Pope claims to be the overseer of the whole world-wide church! He claims to watch over, to shepherd or pastor, more people than any other leader. His look is more stout than others and is greatly feared, for he claims to be the possessor of the keys to the kingdom of heaven.

7. The little horn was to "make *war* with" and "*wear out* the saints of the most High" (Daniel 7:21,25). The early Christians were persecuted by the Jews, later came persecutions under the rule of the pagan Roman Empire. But the war against the saints here described was to be carried out by a power that would rise out of Rome *following* the breaking up of the Empire. Looking into history, we find that century after century of persecution did come upon the saints by a power that rose out of Rome. That power was the Papacy—and none other.

Christians who would not bow to Papal claims, were horribly tortured, tested, and tried during those centuries. Pope Innocent IV issued an official document which stated that these heretics were to be crushed like venomous snakes. His soldiers were promised property and remission of all their sins if they killed a heretic! Victims of the Inquisition were stretched and torn apart on the "rack." Some were crushed and stabbed to death in "iron virgins." There was the thumb-screw, an instrument made for disarticulating the fingers and "Spanish boots" which were used to crush the legs and feet. Pinchers were used to tear out fingernails or were applied red-hot to the sensitive parts of the body.

Every imaginable method of torture was used that fiendish men could imagine. Those who wouldn't bow to the Pope's system were shut up in caves and dungeons,

138

THE INQUISITION—Ridpath's History of the World

were nailed to trees, tormented with fires, scalded with oil or burning pitch; melted lead was poured into their eyes, ears, and mouths; they were scalped, skinned, flayed alive; heads were twisted off and eyes gouged out; women were defiled, their breasts cut off; babies were brutally beaten, whipped, stabbed, dashed against trees—in front of their parents—and then thrown to hungry dogs and swine. It has been estimated that fifty million Christians were killed during those centuries of Papal persecution.

If such treatment as this, inflicted on generation after generation, is not the "wearing out of the saints of the most High," what could be? All other persecutions against the saints were brief and mild in comparison.

Those who hold the futurist interpretation, however, commonly think of the Antichrist as a super-politician who will drop highly destructive bombs from jet planes. As one writer says, Antichrist will "plunge the nations into

139

the last great atomic war."[35] But this is not what the Bible is talking about here. The dropping of bombs upon cities would kill people whether they were saints or sinners. In fact, this kind of war would kill more sinners than saints—for obvious reasons. But the war of Daniel 7 was not to be mass destruction of the people *as a whole*—it was specifically described as war against the *saints!*

8. The little horn would "think to change times and laws" (Daniel 7:25). Daniel said that God is the one that "changeth the times and the seasons" (Daniel 2:21), but this "little horn" dares to even meddle with *divine* things! If he were to merely change civil laws, this would not be too significant—politicians commonly do this. But for him to tamper with divine laws demonstrates his blasphemous character.

As far as human laws, the Papacy has annulled the decrees of kings and emperors; it has thrust its long arm into the affairs of the nations; it has brought rulers to its feet in abject humility. In religious things, the Pope claims infallibility in pronouncing doctrine. By exalting himself to such a position—and millions have believed this dogma—it is evident that he has thought to change divine things. He has instituted the observance of days for which there is no scriptural basis, has instituted rituals and rites that were borrowed directly from paganism, and has set himself up as the final authority on matters of doctrine.

We see, then, that the little horn would be a Roman power, would rise among the ten kingdoms into which the empire was divided, would pluck up three of the other kingdoms, would be diverse, would make great claims, would be a seer, would wear out the saints, and would think to change times and laws.

Understanding this prophecy, the early Christians knew that the Roman Empire—the fourth beast—would be broken up and its fall would bring on the man of sin. Since the man of sin, the little horn of Daniel 7, would make war against the *saints*, Paul concluded that the man of sin would *have* to come to power BEFORE the saints would be gathered at the second coming of Christ! (2 Thessalonians 2:1-3). It all fits together.

Continuing now in Paul's prophecy, we see that he links the man of sin with a falling away. "That day shall not come, except there come a *falling away* first, and that man of sin be revealed..." (2 Thessalonians 2:1-3). The Greek word that is here translated "falling away" is *apostasia*, defined by *Strong's Concordance* as "defection from the truth." It is from this word we get our English word "apostasy." This was not to be a falling away from religion into atheism, but rather a falling away that would develop within the realm of the Christian church. As Lenski has said: "This is apostasy. It is, therefore, to be sought *in* the church visible and not *outside* the church, not in the pagan world, in the general moral decline, in Mohammedanism, in the French Revolution, in the rise and spread of Masonry, in Soviet Russia, or in lesser phenomena."[36]

Has this "falling away" already happened, or is it still in the future? Those who are acquainted with church history know the answer. The original New Testament church was filled with truth and spiritual power. But as time went on, even as the inspired apostles had warned (Acts 20:29,30; 1 Timothy 4:1-3; 2 Peter 2:2,3), there began to be departures from the true faith. The mystery of iniquity was at work. Compromises were made with paganism. Finally, what the world recognized as the "Church" in the fourth and fifth centuries had actually become the *fallen* church. A Biblical and historical account of these things is given in the author's book, *Babylon Mystery Religion*.[37] Only if Christianity had remained doctrinally pure through all the centuries until now, could the apostasy be yet future. This has obviously not been the case.

As the falling away developed, the bishop of Rome rose to power claiming to be "Bishop of bishops," that the whole Christian world should look to him as *head*, and to ROME as *headquarters* for the church. Through the centuries, this apostasy has continued with a "man," at Rome, exalting himself above all others, claiming divine honors and worship—a continual reminder that the falling away took place centuries ago.

Newton has written: "If the apostasy be rightly charged upon the church of Rome, it follows that the man of sin is the pope, not meaning this or that pope in particular, but the pope *in general*, as the chief head and supporter of this apostasy. The apostasy produces him and he promotes the apostasy."[38] Barnes has expressed it this way: "That his [the pope's] rise was preceded by a great apostasy, or departure from the purity of the simple gospel, as revealed in the New Testament, cannot reasonably be doubted by anyone acquainted with the history of the church. That he is the creation or result of that apostasy, is equally clear."[39]

THE TEMPLE OF GOD

According to Paul's prophecy, the man of sin was to "exalt himself above all...in the temple of God" (2 Thessalonians 2:4). Futurists suppose Paul was speaking of a future Jewish temple in Jerusalem. But, unless this verse would be the exception, Paul *never* applied this term to the Jewish temple! Repeatedly he used this expression in reference to believers, to the *church*—never to a literal building:

"Know you not that *you* are the TEMPLE OF GOD, and that the Spirit of God dwells in you? If any man defile the TEMPLE OF GOD, him shall God destroy; for the TEMPLE OF GOD is holy, which temple *you* are" (1 Corinthians 3:16,17). "What? know you not that your body is the TEMPLE of the Holy Ghost which is in you, which you have of God?" (1 Corinthians 6:19). Each believer is as a stone, a living stone, in that great "spiritual house," "the church of the living God" (1 Peter 2:5; 1 Timothy 3:15). "And what agreement hath the TEMPLE OF GOD with idols? For *you* are the TEMPLE OF THE LIVING GOD" (2 Corinthians 6:16). "*You* are built on the foundation of the apostles and prophets, Jesus Christ himself being the chief cornerstone; in whom all the building fitly framed together groweth unto an holy TEMPLE in the Lord: in whom you also are builded together for an habitation of God" (Ephesians 2:20-22). The temple of God is now the church.

The realm, then, in which this man of sin would seek to position himself would be, as Barnes says, "the Christian *church*." To this he adds: "It is by no means necessary to understand this of the temple at Jerusalem....The idea is that the Antichrist would present himself in the midst of the *church* as claiming the honors due

142

to God alone....The authority claimed by the Pope of Rome, meets the full force of the language used here by the apostle."[40]

The man of sin would "sit" in the temple of God "as God," implying he would claim a place of rulership within the church. "Sit" (*kathizo*) implies a "seat" (*kathedra*), from which we derive the word "Cathedral"—the bishop's seat. When the Pope speaks "ex cathedra," he is speaking from his seat officially, such pronouncements being considered infallible. Guinness says: "There, in that exalted cathedral position, and claiming to represent God, the man of sin was to act and abide as the pretended vicar, but the real antagonist, of Christ, undermining His authority, abolishing His laws, and oppressing His people."[41]

The man of sin is further described as he that "exalteth himself above all that is called God, or that is worshipped; so that he *as* God sitteth in the temple of God, showing himself that he is God" (2 Thessalonians 2:4). We understand from this description that the man of sin would exalt himself in great pride, would make great claims, would magnify himself above all others.

Similar expressions are found in various ways through the scriptures. The prince of Tyrus was represented as saying: "I am a God, I sit in the seat of God" (Ezekiel 28:2). The king of Babylon, being lifted up with pride, was represented as saying: "I will exalt my throne above the stars of God...I will be like the most High" (Isaiah 14:4-15). Daniel spoke of one who "shall exalt himself, and magnify himself above every god...for he shall magnify himself above all" (Daniel 11:36,37).

Expressions about leaders exalting themselves unto heaven, exalting themselves above every god, sitting in the seat of God, being like the most High, etc., figuratively describe their pride and arrogance. In the case of the man of sin, he would exalt himself above all others—above all others *in the church!* That is, he would not only claim to be "a" leader in the church, he would actually claim to be "the" leader. The man of sin would claim to be "*as* God," exalting himself as head of the church—a position that belongs only to the Lord himself—"showing that he is God." There is no article before "God" in this case; the meaning is that the man of sin would claim divine attributes. "This expression would not imply that he actually claimed to be the true God," writes Barnes, "but only that he sits in the temple, and manifests himself *as if* he were God. He claims such honors and such reverence as the true God would if he should appear in human form."[42]

Have the popes claimed to be above all *that* is called God, have they claimed to be *as God* in the temple of God, and have they attempted to show that they are *divine?* Yes. They have claimed to be above all kings and emperors. They have claimed not only the rule of earth, but heaven and hell also. They have claimed attributes and titles which can rightly pertain only to God. At the coronation of

Pope Innocent X, the following words were addressed to him by a cardinal who knelt before him: "Most holy and blessed father! head of the Church, ruler of the world, to whom the keys of the kingdom of heaven are committed, whom the angels in heaven revere, and the gates of hell fear, and all the world adores, we specially venerate, worship, and adore thee!"

Moreri, a noted historian, wrote: "To make war against the Pope is to make war against God, seeing the Pope *is God* and God is the Pope." Decius said: "The Pope can do all things God can do." Pope Leo XIII said of himself in

144

1890: "The supreme teacher in the Church is the Roman Pontiff. Union of minds, therefore, requires, together with a perfect accord in the one faith, complete submission and obedience of will to the Church and to the Roman Pontiff, *as to God himself.*" In 1894, he said: "We hold the place of Almighty God on earth."

On April 30, 1922, in the Vatican throne room before a throng of cardinals, bishops, priests, and nuns, who fell on their knees before him, Pope Pius XI in haughty tones said: "You know that I am the Holy Father, the representative of God on earth, the Vicar of Christ, which means that *I am God* on the earth."

The pagan Caesar was called "our Lord and God." For centuries the popes accepted the same title. On the arch raised in honor of Pope Borgia were the words: "Rome was great under Caesar; now she is greater: Alexander VI reigns. The former was a man: this is a *god"!* Pope Pius X, when Archbishop of Venice, said: "The Pope is not only the representative of Jesus Christ, he *is* Jesus Christ himself, hidden under the veil of the flesh. Does the Pope speak? It is Jesus Christ who speaks."

The following is an extract from actual wording that has been used by popes:

"The Roman Pontiff judges all men, but is judged by no one....We declare...to be subject to the Roman Pontiff is to every creature altogether *necessary for salvation.* ...That which was spoken of Christ, 'Thou has subdued all things under his feet' may well seem verified in me...I have the authority of the King of kings. I am all in all and *above all...*I am able to do almost all that God can do....Wherefore if those things that I do be said not to be done of man but of God: what can you make me but *God?...*Wherefore no marvel if it be in my power *to change time and times,* to alter and abrogate *laws,* to dispense with all things, yea, with the precepts of *Christ;* for where Christ biddeth Peter to put up his sword and admonishes his disciples not to use any outward force in revenging themselves, so do not I, Pope Nicholas, writing to the Bishops of France, exhort them to draw out their material swords?...Wherefore, as I began, so I conclude, commanding, declaring, and pronouncing, to stand upon necessity of salvation, for every creature to be subject to *me,*" etc.[43]

The man of sin is referred to as "the son of perdition" (2 Thessalonians 2:3). This same title was applied to Judas Iscariot (John 17:12). By this duplication of the term, the Holy Spirit is apparently showing that the man of sin would resemble Judas. To outward appearances, Judas was a bishop and apostle (Acts 1:20,25). Nevertheless, he "was a thief, and had the bag, and bare what was put therein" (John 12:6). Such words could well describe papal practices, especially during the Dark Ages. Though Judas had received thirty pieces of silver to betray Jesus, he approached him in the garden with a kiss and the words, "Hail Master"! So also has the Papacy claimed to be Christ's apostle and friend, but has betrayed him by promoting doctrines and practices that are contrary to what he taught—indulgence selling, prayers for the dead in purgatory, payment for masses, relic sales, offerings before idols, etc.

The man of sin's rise to power was to be accompanied by claims of supernatural signs and wonders. "Whose coming is after [according to] the working of Satan with all power and signs and lying wonders" (2 Thessalonians 2:9). A full account of all the miracles which have supposedly happened within this system would fill volumes: crucifixes have spoken; images have come down and lit their own candles; idols have sweat, turned their eyes, moved their hands, opened their mouths, healed sicknesses, raised the dead, mended broken bones; souls from purgatory have appeared on lonely roads and begged that masses be said in their behalf; many have claimed that the virgin Mary visited them, etc. All of these miracles—whether supposed, real, or faked—greatly increased the fallen church.

We see, then, that the man of sin would appear in connection with the falling away; he would rise to power within the very framework of Christianity, claiming to be above all others, as God; his rise to power would be accompanied with lying signs and wonders. We have seen evidence, point by point, that these things did find fulfillment in the Papacy.

Some object to this interpretation on the basis that Paul spoke of "*the* man of sin"—meaning an individual man, not a succession of men. But this is not necessarily true. "The" is used in the expression *"the* man of God" (2 Timothy 3:16)—a reference to a *class* of men of certain character, a succession of *similar* individuals. Or we read about *"the* high priest" (Hebrews 9:7)—meaning a *succession* of high priests. The church—the long line or succession of believers through the centuries—is spoken of as *"one* new man" (Ephesians 2:15). A single beast in prophecy often represents a whole empire or kingdom in all its changes and revolutions from beginning to end. The four beasts of Daniel 7 are mentioned as four kings, yet the meaning is not limited to individual kings, for each of these kingdoms included a *succession* of rulers.

Grammatically, the expression "the man of sin" could mean either an individual *or* a succession of similar individuals. There is a strong hint, however, that a succession of men is meant. "He that *letteth"* was a line or succession of Caesars, so it would not be inconsistent to believe "he that *sitteth"* would also be a succession of men. Even so, the idea of *one* man is not eliminated by this interpretation, for there is only *one man at a time* who occupies the papal office.

Something else should be considered here—the statement that the little horn would "wear out the saints of the most High" for "a time and times and the dividing of time" (Daniel 7:25). The early Christians, not knowing the times and seasons (Acts 1:7), had no way to determine that time would continue on for at least another 2,000 years. Consequently, from their prospective, they may have believed the fall of the Roman Empire would be sudden, that Antichrist would be an individual who would rise to power, and that he would wear out the saints for a literal three and a half years. Centuries later, when the light of the Reformation revived the study of prophecy, many Christians came to see that these prophecies had indeed been fulfilled, though on a somewhat longer scale than might have been originally understood.

Rome had fallen, but it was a decline and fall—taking place over a period of years. The rise of the Papacy was also gradual—many years passing before it met all the requirements of the prophecy. The time, times, and dividing of time—three and a half years or 1260 days—during which the little horn would "wear out the saints," was understood by many expositors on the year-for-a-day principle; that is, 1260 years. In fact, the Papacy did wear out the saints century after century during the period known as the Dark Ages, during which, it is believed, over 50 million were tortured and killed.

It has been said that prophecy is a wonderful combination of the clear and the obscure; enough to show the hand of God, but not enough to make fatalists of the readers; enough to prove the message to have been from God, but not enough to enable man to know all the details of how that purpose is to be realized. We believe this has been the case with the prophecy about the man of sin.

JOHN'S PROPHECY—THE ANTICHRIST

We turn now to the writings of John, the only Biblical writer who actually uses the word "Antichrist." Writing at a time when many novel doctrines were making the rounds, the burden of John's message was for Christians to hold the original faith as taught at the *beginning:*

> "That which was from the *beginning,* which we have heard [from Christ]...declare we unto you....This then is the message which we have heard of him, and declare unto you" (1 John 1:1-5). He speaks of the instruction they "had from the *beginning*" and the word which they had "heard from the *beginning*" (2:7). "Let that therefore abide in you which you have heard from the *beginning.* If that which you have heard from the *beginning* shall remain in you, you also shall continue in the Son, and in the Father" (2:24); "the message that you heard from the *beginning*" (3:11). He mentions "that which we had from the *beginning*" (2 John 5) and "as you have heard from the *beginning,* you should walk in it" (verse 6).

The reason John placed this strong emphasis on that which was taught "at the beginning," was because many had departed from the original faith into false doctrines. These who had departed he termed "antichrists."

> "Little children...you have heard that ANTICHRIST shall come, even now are there many antichrists....They went *out from us...*" (1 John 2:18,19).

148

These "antichrists"—a type of the Antichrist that was to come—were not atheists! They were people who professed to be Christians. We agree with the Scofield note: "'Went out from us,' that is, *doctrinally*. Doubtless then, as now, the deniers of the Son still called themselves Christians."[44] If, then, the ones that John used as a type of the Antichrist that was to come were *professing* Christians —but who had departed into erroneous doctrines—why should we look for Antichrist somewhere outside the realm of professing Christianity? Even Scofield, in at least one note, said: "The 'little horn' is an apostate...*from Christianity*, not Judaism."[45]

The next "Antichrist" passage is 1 John 2:22-26:

> Who is a liar but he that *denieth* that Jesus is the Christ? He is ANTICHRIST, that *denieth* the Father and the Son. Whosoever *denieth* the Son, the same hath not the Father....Let that therefore abide in you, which you have heard from the *beginning*. If that which you have heard from the *beginning* shall remain in you, you also shall continue in the Son and in the Father....These things have I written unto you concerning them that *seduce* you (1 John 2:22-26).

Again, those who taught things contrary to that which was from the beginning, were termed "antichrist." By teaching such things, they *denied* the Father and the Son. But it was not a barefaced denial, for John mentions the *seductive* nature of these teachings. Some, upon reading the word "denied," assume the Antichrist will be an atheist—one who denies the *existence* of God—or at least an infidel! We hear talk about Antichrist being "the World's number one ATHEIST,"[46] or that "the blasphemy of the little horn seems...to be downright, barefaced INFIDELITY."[47] But the early Christians never heard of an *infidel* Antichrist. Apparently this idea was first taught in a *ninth century* commentary by Berengaud.[48]

Fred Peters has written: "When we teach that the Papacy (the dynasty of popes) is the Antichrist, in common with all the great Reformers and Protestants for 1000 years past, we are often told...that the Antichrist has to be an unbeliever, an atheist, an infidel, which the Pope is not. Thus with a wave of the hand is the mighty prophetic teaching, that shook the Papacy to its foundation, dis-

149

missed....Often an earnest seeker asks of some futurist preacher if the Pope is the Antichrist of the Bible, and the matter is settled in a minute, in the most superficial way, by saying, 'No, for he does not *deny* the Father and the Son'...and that ends the subject, for the seeker does not seek further along that line, unless he has a firm resolve to know all the truth, and why the old Reformers and Protestants thus taught."[49]

Those "antichrists" that John mentioned were not atheists, but professing Christians. Their teachings were "seducing" Christians into counterfeit doctrines. Teaching atheism would not have this seductive effect, for it does not even pretend to be a Christian doctrine. What, then, is meant by the statement that they *denied* the Father and the Son? It was not that they denied the existence of God. They denied him in other ways—mainly by claiming to be Christians, yet adhering to false doctrines which were not the original teachings of the church. This point becomes clear when we see how this word "deny" was used *in the scriptures.*

1. Jude, like John, wrote of the apostasy that was creeping in: "It was needful for me to write unto you, and exhort you that you should earnestly contend for *the* faith that was once delivered unto the saints." Why? "For there are certain men crept in *unawares*...turning the grace of our God into lasciviousness, and DENYING the only Lord God, and our Lord Jesus Christ" (Jude 3,4). Notice that these false teachers were so deceptive with their novel doctrines that they "crept in unawares." By their erroneous and counterfeit doctrines, they *denied* the Lord! Nothing is said that would indicate these apostates denied the *existence* of God. If they had come in among the Christians denying the existence of God, in no way could they have come in unawares.

2. Peter likewise wrote of apostasy that would develop within the church. "There shall be false teachers *among you,* who privily [secretly, in a hidden way] shall bring in damnable heresies, even DENYING the Lord that *bought* them...and many shall follow their pernicious ways" (2 Peter 2:1,2). Clearly these false teachers were not denying the existence of God, for that would not deceive those

150

Christians to whom Peter wrote. The way they denied him was by teaching erroneous and deceptive doctrines. On an earlier occasion, Peter said that the Jews delivered up Christ "and DENIED him in the presence of Pilate...they DENIED the Holy One and the Just...and killed the Prince of life, whom God hath raised from the dead" (Acts 3:13-15). The ones who denied Christ did not deny his *existence*. They denied him by rejecting his claims and having him crucified.

3. Paul used the word "deny" in connection with those who taught false doctrines among Christians. They are mentioned as "deceivers...who subvert whole houses, teaching things which thy ought not." Such were not "sound in the faith"; but gave heed to doctrines that cause men to "turn from the truth....They profess that they know God; but in works they DENY him, being abominable, and disobedient" (Titus 1:10-16).

Having considered the word "denied" as used by Jude, Peter, Paul, and John, it is clear that atheism is not meant. Those who denied the Lord did so by not fully following the original Christian faith in word and deed. These were called "antichrists."

Our next "antichrist" passage is 1 John 4:1-6:

> Beloved, believe not every spirit, but try the spirits whether they are of God: because many *false prophets* are gone out into the world...every spirit that confesseth not that Jesus Christ is come in the flesh is not of God: and this is that spirit of ANTICHRIST, whereof you have heard that it should come; and even now already is it in the world....They are of the world....We are of God: he that knoweth God heareth *us* [the apostles]; he that is not of God heareth not us. Hereby know we the spirit of truth, and the spirit of error.

Since John and the other apostles had received their message *from Christ himself*, he could say that those who believed their message were of God. Those who did not stand for the apostolic faith were "false prophets," their inspiration not coming from the Holy Spirit, but the antichrist spirit. John was not dealing here with such things as political corruption, alcoholism, prostitution, brutality, or crime in the streets. Christians could easily recognize

151

these for what they were. What John dealt with here was the *deception* of counterfeit doctrines.

John warned the people to continue in the truth "as you have heard from the beginning"—the apostolic doctrine—*"for* many deceivers are entered into the world, who confess not that Jesus Christ is come in the flesh. This is a *deceiver* and an ANTICHRIST...whosoever abideth not in the doctrine of Christ, hath not God. He that abideth in the doctrine of Christ, he hath both the Father and the Son" (2 John 7-9).

Whatever this particular teaching may have been—that Jesus had not come "in the flesh"—it was not a denial of the *existence* of Christ (for this would not *deceive* Christians). Instead, it was apparently an erroneous and counterfeit view regarding his incarnation in the flesh. Consider the following:

The Ebionites, according to Irenaeus, taught that Christ was not born by a supernatural conception, but regarded him as a mere man. The Gnostics called in question the reality of Christ's human nature, believing the historical Christ was a mask of the real Christ, the heavenly Christ, not Christ incarnate in flesh. The followers of Cerinthus believed there was a distinction between the heavenly Christ and Jesus of Nazareth—that the two were connected in a temporary union. The Docetists taught that Christ's body was merely a phantom, not actually human flesh. The Theodotians considered Christ only as a man. The Adoptionists and the Followers of Paul of Samosata thought that Jesus had been born a man, but achieved divinity through moral perfection.

Though all of these groups taught false views concerning the incarnation of Christ in the flesh, none of them were atheists. They were "antichrists" because they had departed from the faith that was taught "at the beginning." The fact that John especially mentioned a prominent false doctrine *of that time*—the teaching that Jesus had not come in the flesh—does not infer that Antichrist would be *limited* in his denial to the same doctrines that those apostates held. Neither those who hold the futurist view or those who hold the fulfilled view, limit the errors of Antichrist to this one point of doctrine.

152

Some suppose John's use of the word "antichrist" simply means a person *against* Christ. But millions of people have been *against* Christ. Paul, before his conversion, was against Christ. Jews, pagans, and members of non-Christian religions in varying degrees have all been against Christ. However, if John used the word "antichrists" concerning people who professed to be Christians—but who were against Christ because of their false doctrines—we have *a very specific point of identification!* Since *these* "antichrists" were a type of the Antichrist to come, there is a very strong inference that Antichrist would profess to be a Christian, supposedly *for* Christ, yet actually *against* him because of false doctrine.

It is well established that the word "antichrist" can mean (1) *against* [in opposition] to Christ, (2) *instead of* [in the place of] Christ, or (3) *both* meanings. As Elliott has written: "When *anti* is compounded with the noun signifying an agent of any kind, or functionary, the compound word either signifies a vice-functionary, or a functionary of the same kind opposing, or sometimes both."[50]

An example of the word having both meanings is found right within the terminology of the Roman Catholic Church. At times two men would claim to be pope. The one who was considered a hostile, self-substituted, usurping pope, was called an "antipope." Such a "pope" positioned himself *in place of* the Pope, *as* the pope, but was, as such, *against* the Pope—thus an "antipope." For a man, then, to claim to be the head of the church, *in place of* Christ, what is this but to be, in reality, *against* Christ—or ANTICHRIST? The reason for this is simple: CHRIST *alone* is the head of the church (Ephesians 1:22; 4:15; 5:23; Colossians 1:18).

Porcelli has written that the very title which the Pope bears, "Vicar of Christ," can only be turned into Greek as "Antichristos"—that is, the Vice-christ, substitute Christ, or Antichrist![51] Thus have the popes claimed a title which is the equivalent of the word coined by John!

As those "antichrists" of whom John spoke, so have the Popes denied the Lord by promoting false doctrines that cause men to err from the truth. They have even

153

dared to oppose Christ by teaching things that are the exact *opposite* of what Christ and the apostles taught!

OPPOSITES

1. *Prayer.* "When you pray, use not vain *repetitions,* as the heathen do: for they think that they shall be heard for their much speaking" (Matthew 6:7). Those who look to the Pope as head of the church repeat prayers over and over such as the Hail Mary: "Hail Mary, full of grace, the Lord is with thee; Blessed art thou among women, and blessed is the fruit of thy womb, Jesus. Holy Mary, Mother of God, pray for us sinners, now and at the hour of death, Amen." In reciting the Rosary, this prayer is repeated 53 times.

2. *Treasures.* "Lay not up for yourselves *treasures* upon earth" (Matthew 6:19). The Papal church has done just the opposite. Consider the wealth and treasures that are contained within the Vatican. Some of the jewel-covered crowns worn by the popes have been valued at over a million dollars. Consider the massive cathedrals and churches around the world, many of which are lavishly decorated with silver and gold. In Mexico we have seen expensive cathedrals of elaborate proportions with idols and altars of gold—while many of the poor people all around them live in mud huts and shacks. If there has ever been a corporation or system that has laid up treasures, it has been the Roman Catholic Church—in direct conflict with what Jesus taught.

3. *Love.* "Whosoever shall smite you on your right cheek, turn to him the other also...*love* your enemies, bless them that curse you, do good to them that hate you, and pray for them which despitefully use you, and persecute you" (Matthew 5:39,44). In direct contrast to this, the Papacy promoted the horrid inquisition in which Protestants were to be "crushed like venomous snakes." Every conceivable method of torture was used upon those who would not bow to the Papal claims.

4. *Father.* "Call no man your *father* upon the earth: for one is your Father, which is in heaven" (Matthew 23:9). Though Jesus spoke against the use of flattering religious titles, people of the Papal church constantly use the unscriptural title of "father" when addressing priests.

154

5. *Marriage.* "A bishop then must be blameless, the husband of one wife" (1 Timothy 3:2). Ministers in the New Testament church, including Peter, were married (Matthew 8:14; 1 Corinthians 9:5). The doctrine of "forbidding to marry" was considered a doctrine of devils by the early church (1 Timothy 4:1-3). But, as is well known, for centuries the Papal church has insisted on priestly celibacy.

6. *Idols and images.* "Keep yourselves from *idols*" (1 John 5:21). Have the people of the Papal church obeyed this? They have not. On the walls of their homes, on the dashboards of their cars, on medals suspended from their necks, in their churches, and at roadside shrines—everywhere, and in multiplied ways, the use of idols and images is encouraged and promoted. The early church never used images of Christ, Mary, and saints in their worship.

7. *Scriptures.* The Bible commends people who study the scriptures (Acts 17:11), but the Roman Catholic church for centuries opposed Bible study. Pope Pius IV stated: "The Bible is not for the people; whosoever will be saved must renounce it. It is a forbidden book. Bible societies are Satanic contrivances."

In 860, Pope Nicholas I put Bible reading under the ban as did Gregory VII in 1073. In 1198 Innocent III issued a decree that all who read the Bible should be put to death. In 1229 the Council of Tolouse passed a decree forbidding either the possession or reading of the Bible, as did also the famous Council of Trent. Pius VII in 1816 denounced Bibles as "pestilences." Gregory XVI in 1844 condemned Bible societies and ordered priests to tear up all they could lay their hands on.

We believe all of these things argue strongly that the Papacy, though claiming to represent Christ, has in a definite sense *opposed* Christ. Taking, then, the evidence we have seen in the writings of Daniel, Paul, and John, we notice the following things:

1. As to TIME, the appearance of the man of sin was to occur when that which was restraining would be taken out of the way. We have seen the reasons for believing this restraint was the Roman Empire and that upon its fall the Papacy did rise to power.

2. As to PLACE, the man of sin would come to power in the place from which the Caesar would be "taken out of the way"; that is, Rome. He would be a Roman power.

3. As to RELIGION, the man of sin would exalt himself above all others in the church—not just as *a* leader, but as THE leader or head of the church. Thus, positioning himself *in the place of* Christ, he would be *against* Christ—Antichrist.

According to the scriptures, Antichrist was to be a ROMAN power and yet he would exalt himself above all others in the fallen CHURCH. Put these two terms together and we have ROMAN CHURCH. We know from history that when the falling away came, it centered at Rome. We need, then, only to ask what "man" rose to head this system and we have identified the man of sin!

Though the picture did not become complete *all at once*, the passing of time thoroughly demonstrated that the Papacy did become a persecuting power, did wear out the saints, did make blasphemous claims, did the things that the prophecies said the Antichrist would do.

Froom has written: "In the centuries just preceding the Reformation an ever-increasing number of pious persons began openly to express the conviction that the dire prophecies concerning Antichrist were even then in the process of fulfillment. They felt that the 'falling away' had *already* taken place. They declared that Antichrist was *already* seated in the churchly temple of God, clothed in scarlet and purple."[52]

TESTIMONY OF MARTYRS AND REFORMERS

EBERHARD II, archbishop of Salzburg (1200-1246), set forth the teaching that the little horn of Daniel 7 was the Pope, that the Pope was a wolf in shepherd's garb, the Antichrist, the son of perdition. He did not look forward to the coming of an unidentified *individual* Antichrist. Instead, he looked back over the centuries since Rome's dismemberment and saw in the historical Papacy, as a system or succession, the fulfillment of the prophecies concerning Antichrist. He was excommunicated by the Pope and died under the ban in 1246.[53]

156

JOHN FOXE, noted writer of *Foxe's Book of Martyrs,* gives a list of learned men between 1331 and 1360 who contended against the false claims of the Pope. One of these, Michael of Cesena, who had numerous followers, not a few of whom were slain, declared the Pope "to be Antichrist, and the church of Rome to be the whore of Babylon, drunk with the blood of the saints."[54]

JOHN WYCLIF (sometimes spelled Wycliffe), noted English Reformer, taught that the persecuting little horn of Daniel had found fulfillment in the Papacy which arose out of the fourth kingdom, Rome. "Why is it necessary in unbelief to look for another Antichrist?" he asked. "In the Seventh Chapter of Daniel, Antichrist is forcefully described by a horn arising in the time of the fourth kingdom...wearing out the saints of the most high."[55] His book, *The Mirror of Antichrist,* is filled with references to the Pope as Antichrist.

From the ministry of Wyclif sprang the English Lollards which numbered in the hundreds of thousands. We give their testimony in the words of one of them, Lord Cobham. When brought before King Henry V and admonished to submit to the Pope as an obedient child, Cobham replied: "As touching the Pope and his spirituality, I owe him neither suit nor service, forasmuch as I know him by the scriptures to be the great Antichrist, the son of perdition."[56] This was a century before Luther.

WALTER BRUTE, noted scholar, prophetic expositor, and associate of Wyclif, was accused in 1391 of oftentimes and commonly claiming that "the Pope is Antichrist and a seducer of the people."[57]

SIR JOHN OLDCASTLE (1360-1417), famous Christian of Herefordshire, spoke of the Pope in these words: "I know him by the scriptures to be the great Antichrist, the son of perdition....Rome is the very nest of Antichrist, and out of that nest come all the disciples of him." He was sentenced to death for naming Antichrist. Though the sentence was not immediately carried out, in 1417 he was dragged to St.

Giles, suspended in chains, and slowly burned to death, as his voice ascended in praise to God.[58]

JOHN HUSS (1369-1415), born in Bohemia, was a well educated man who came under the influence of Wyclif's writings which caused him to break with the church of Rome. He labeled the Pope as the Antichrist of which the scriptures had warned. His writings constantly refer to Antichrist as the enemy of the church—not as a Jew, a pagan, or a Turk—but as a false confessor of the name of Christ. Pope Martin V issued a bull in 1418 in which he ordered the punishment of men or women who held to the teachings of Wyclif and Huss. Sixty miles from Prague, on a steep mountain, the city of Tabor was built to which the "Huss-ites" could "flee from Antichrist."[59]

Huss himself was condemned as a heretic and delivered to the secular arm for execution. Accompanied by a guard of one thousand armed men and a vast crowd of spectators, he was led through the churchyard where he saw a bonfire of his books in the public square. As he knelt and prayed, his hands were tied behind him and a rusty chain was wound round his neck. Straw and wood were piled around him. The name Huss meant "goose" in the Bohemian tongue and at the place of execution Huss reportedly said: "This day ye are burning a *goose;* but from my ashes will arise a *swan,* which ye will not be able to roast"—an expression later quoted by Luther. "Huss began to sing," writes Froom, "but the wind swept the flames into his face and silenced his words. Only his lips moved—until they too were stilled in death for his stand against the Antichrist of Bible prophecy"![60]

MARTIN LUTHER (1483-1546), while still a priest of the Roman Catholic church, disagreed with the practice of selling indulgences. At first, he sought a reform within the church. But as he grew in the knowledge of Christ, he saw that reform would be impossible and that the message was to "come out of her." Being loosened from the bondage of this system, he began to wonder if the Pope was the Antichrist. Eventually this belief became pronounced.

Luther's friends, fearing for his safety, begged him to suppress his book *To the German Nobility.* To this he replied on August 18, 1520: "We here are of the conviction that the Papacy is the seat of the true and real Antichrist...personally I declare that I owe the Pope no other obedience than that to Antichrist."[61] Two months later, Luther's book, *On the Babylonian Captivity of the Church,* was published. In this he spoke of the Papacy (the system, not the individual pope) as "nothing else than the kingdom of Babylon and of very Antichrist....For who is the man of sin and the son of perdition, but he who by his teaching and his ordinances increases the sin and perdition of souls in the church; while he yet sits in the church as if he were God? All these conditions have now for many ages been fulfilled by the papal tyranny."[62]

In 1540, Luther wrote: "Oh, Christ, my Lord, look down upon us and bring upon us thy day of judgment, and destroy the brood of Satan in Rome. There sits the Man, of whom the apostle Paul wrote (2 Thessalonians 2:3,4) that he will oppose and exalt himself above all that is called God—the man of sin, that son of perdition...he suppresses the law of God and exalts his commandments above the commandments of God."[63]

To Luther, the scriptures did not portray Antichrist as an infidel, or a super-politician, but as one that would rise within the church realm; that is, "in the midst of Christendom." Concerning the man of sin, he pointed out that he "sitteth not in a stable of fiends, or in a swine-sty, or in a company of infidels, but in the highest and holiest place of all, namely, in the temple of God....Is not this to sit in the temple of God, to profess himself to be the Ruler in the whole church? What is the temple of God? Is it stones and wood? Did not Paul say, The temple of God is holy, which temple you are? To sit—what is it but to reign, to teach, and to judge? Who from the beginning of the church has dared to call himself master of the whole church but the Pope alone? None of the saints, none of the heretics ever uttered so horrible a word of pride."[64]

It is evident that Luther did not believe the Antichrist would be some lone individual at the end of time, for he said: "The Antichrist of whom Paul speaks *now reigns* in the court of Rome." As the *Encyclopedia Britannica* says, "These ideas became the dynamic force which drove Luther on in his contest with the Papacy."[65]

Among other leaders with Luther in the Reformation in Germany was ANDREAS OSIANDER (1498-1552), who also took a stand against the Roman Antichrist who spoke words against God and who had seated himself in God's temple. His concept of Antichrist was not limited to one individual man. He believed it was the Papal ecclesiastical *system* which rose with the fall of Rome and would extend until the end time. He felt that the Papal contention that the Antichrist was some *future* person had caused people to look ahead for a fictitious Antichrist and thus overlook the *real* Antichrist at Rome who had already exerted his influence for centuries.[66]

NICOLAUS VON AMSDORF (1483-1565), a close friend and zealous co-worker of Luther, believed that the Antichrist was to rise within the church realm and that "the Pope is the real, true Antichrist and not the vicar of Christ."[67]

PHILIPP MELANCHTHON (1497-1560), who was also associated with Luther, identified Antichrist in this way:

"Since it is certain that the pontiffs and the monks have forbidden marriage [cf. 1 Timothy 4:1-3], it is most manifest, and true without any doubt, that the Roman Pontiff, with his whole order and kingdom, is very Antichrist....Likewise in 2 Thessalonians 2, Paul clearly says that the man of sin will rule in the church exalting himself above the worship of God."[68]

Generally regarded as second only to Luther in influence is the eminent French reformer JOHN CALVIN (1509-1564). Originally a son of the Papal church, about 1532 he embraced the Protestant faith. His published works fill some fifty volumes. Concerning the Pope, he said: "I deny him to be the vicar of Christ, who, in furiously persecuting the gospel, demonstrates by his con-

duct that he is Antichrist—I deny him to be the successor of Peter...I deny him to be the head of the church."[69] In his classic *Institutes* he wrote:

"Some persons think us too severe and censorious when we call the Roman pontiff Antichrist. But those who are of this opinion do not consider that they bring the same charge of presumption against Paul himself, after whom we speak and whose language we adopt....I shall briefly show that [Paul's words in 2 Thessalonians 2] are not capable of *any other interpretation* than that which applies them to the *Papacy.*" He then pointed out that the Antichrist was to conceal himself under the character of the church, "as under a mask," and that the Papacy had fulfilled the characteristics set forth by Paul.

JOHN KNOX (1505-1572), especially known for his reformation work in Scotland, was persecuted from country to country until finally the affairs of Scotland were in Protestant hands. He preached that Romish traditions and ceremonies should be abolished as well as "that tyranny which the Pope himself has for so many ages

exercised over the church" and that he should be acknowledged as "the very Antichrist, the son of perdition, of whom Paul speaks."[70] In public challenge, Knox said: "As for your Roman Church, as it is now corrupted...I no more doubt but that it is the synagogue of Satan, and the head thereof, called the Pope, to be that man of sin of whom the apostle speaketh."

HULDREICH ZWINGLI (1484-1531) was a prominent figure in the work of the reformation that broke out in Switzerland. On December 28, 1524, he very wisely pointed out that the Papacy was evil, but that it must be overthrown by the preaching of the word in love and never by hatred: "I know that in it works the might and power of the Devil, that is, of the Antichrist...the Papacy has  to be abolished....But by no other means can it be more thoroughly routed than by the word of God (2 Thessalonians 2), because as soon as the world receives this in the right way, it will turn away from the Pope without compulsion."[71]

HEINRICH BULLINGER (1504-1575), friend of Zwingli, is regarded as one of the greatest prophetic expositors of the time. He explained that the kingdom of the popes rose up among the divisions of Rome, that the Pope is Antichrist because he usurps the keys of Christ and his kingly and priestly authority.[72]

THEODOR BIBLIANDER (1504-1564), called the "Father of Biblical Exegesis in Switzerland," a noted translator and Bible scholar, declared that the Papacy is the Antichrist predicted in 2 Thessalonians 2.[73]

ALFONSUS CONRADUS who fled from Italy to Switzerland because of his religious convictions, wrote a large commentary in 1560 on the book of Revelation in which he taught that the Roman Papacy is the Antichrist. He said it was useless to wait for the coming of Antichrist in the future, for he had *already* been revealed.[74]

JOHN NAPIER (1550-1617), noted Scottish mathematician and adherent of the Protestant cause, wrote a commentary on Revelation which the *Encyclopedia Britannica* refers to as the first important Scottish work on the interpretation of scripture. He taught that the Antichrist was the Pope—and not a Turk, a Jew, or someone outside the church realm—for he "must sit, saith Paul, in the church of God."[75]

WILLIAM TYNDALE (1484-1536), first translator of the Bible from Greek to English, reformer and martyr, held that the Papal church was Babylon and that the Pope was the man of sin or Antichrist, seated in the temple of God, i.e., the church. Repeatedly he cited 2 Thessalonians 2 in this connection.[76]

Years later (in 1611), the translators of the King James Version also recognized the Papacy as the man of sin, and that the open publication of scriptural truth was dealing a great blow to him. Thus they wrote in their dedication to King James: "...the zeal of your majesty toward the house of God doth not slack or go backward but is more and more kindled, manifesting itself abroad in the fartherest parts of Christendom by writing a defence of the truth which *hath given such a blow to that man of sin* as will not be healed." It is evident these men did not think the man of sin was an individual to be revealed at some *future* time!

KING JAMES (1566-1625) himself believed that following the removal of the Roman emperors, the reign of Antichrist began. This was, of course, a reference to the rise of the Papacy which he believed to be the Antichrist and Mystery of Iniquity.[77]

NICHOLAS RIDLEY (1500-1555), a well known English martyr and man of great learning, memorized most of the epistles in Greek and wrote numerous works. He spoke out on the deceptions of Romanism and that "the head,

under Satan, of all mischief is Antichrist and his brood." Before his martyrdom on October 16, 1555, he wrote a farewell in which he said goodbye to his wife, relatives, and friends. He gave a review of his faith and spoke of how the Papacy had developed over the centuries. He described Rome as "the seat of Satan; and the bishop of the same, that maintains the abominations thereof, is Antichrist himself indeed."[78]

A friend of Ridley, JOHN BRADFORD (1510-1555), a noted preacher, was also martyred for his Protestant stand. On June 30, 1555, he was taken from prison late at night, all the prisoners tearfully bidding him farewell. As he passed along, great crowds were waiting, many weeping and praying for him. Standing by the stake where he would be killed, he raised both hands and called England to repentance. He wrote a farewell in which he declared that he was condemned "for not acknowledging the Antichrist of Rome to be Christ's vicar-general and supreme head of the Catholic and universal church." He spoke of the Papacy as being *"undoubtedly* that great Antichrist, of whom the apostles do so much admonish us."[79]

THOMAS CRANMER (1489-1556), writing in 1550, said of the Papacy: "I know how Antichrist hath obscured the glory of God, and the true knowledge of his word, overcasting the same with mists and clouds of error and ignorance through false glosses and interpretation....Antichrist of Rome...hath extolled himself above his fellow bishops, as God's vicar, yea, rather as God himself; and taketh upon him authority over kings and emperors, and sitteth in the temple of God, that is, in the consciences of men, and causeth his decrees to be more regarded than God's laws; yea, and for money he dispenseth with God's laws...giving men license to break them."[80] After quoting from the prophecies of Daniel and Revelation, he said: "Whereof it fol-

loweth Rome to be the seat of Antichrist, and the Pope to be very Antichrist himself. I could prove the same by many other scriptures, old writers, and strong reasons."[81]

In his final testimony, he spoke of the Pope as Antichrist, and having said a few more words, was led to the fire which left him a blackened corpse.

JOHN HOOPER (1495-1555) was one of the first arrested for his protestant faith when Mary came to the throne in England. He was condemned because he would not accept the "wicked papistical religion of the bishop of Rome." As a throng of 7,000 gathered—many of them weeping—Hooper was bound to a stake and slowly burned while he prayed. He believed that the so-called Vicar of Christ was in fact the great and principal *enemy* of Christ, that in him were found the very properties of the Antichrist, and that these things were *openly known* to all men that were not blinded with the smoke of Rome.[82]

THOMAS BECON (1511-1567), author of numerous books on popery, wrote: "We desire of our heavenly Father, that Antichrist with his kingdom, which hath seduced, and daily doth seduce...may shortly be slain and brought into confusion 'with the breath of the Lord's mouth'...that 'that sinful man, the son of perdition, which is an adversary, and is exalted above all that is called God, or that is worshipped,' may no longer 'sit in the temple of God, boasting himself to be God'."[83]

HUGH LATIMER (1490-1555) was a fervent preacher with no time for hypocrisy or tyranny. In commenting on the words of Paul in 2 Thessalonians 2, he said in 1552: "The Lord will not come till 'the swerving from faith cometh': which thing is already done and *past.*" The falling away was not some future thing to Latimer. Nor was the man of sin an individual yet to come, for speaking of his day, he said: "Antichrist *is* known throughout all the world."[84]

One of the great intellectuals of the English reformation was JOHN JEWEL (1522-1571). He listed some of the misconceptions held by the Roman Catholic church as to Antichrist: that he would be a Jew of the tribe of Dan, born in Babylonia or Syria, or Mohammed, or that he would overthrow Rome or rebuild Jerusalem. "These tales have been craftily devised to beguile our eyes, that, whilst we think upon these guesses, and so occupy ourselves in beholding a shadow or probable conjecture of Antichrist, he which *is* Antichrist indeed may unawares deceive us." He was referring to the Papacy.

He then mentions that if we took the term "man of sin" by itself, we might suppose that an individual man is meant. But taking all of the evidence into consideration, we understand that a *succession* of men is the proper meaning. He pointed out that pagan Rome was the hindering power that prevented the development of Antichrist and that "Paul saith, Antichrist shall not come yet; for the emperor letteth him: the emperor shall be removed; and then shall Antichrist come." This system of apostasy shall continue until it is destroyed at the Lord's coming. "He meaneth not, therefore, that Antichrist shall be any one man only, but one estate or kingdom of men, and a continuance of some one power and tyranny in the church."[85]

Jewel mentioned some of the Papal claims: that the Pope is lord over all the world, king of kings, and that every knee should bow to him; that his authority reaches into heaven and down into hell; that he can command the angels of God; that he can forgive sins. "This is Antichrist. This is his power. Thus shall he work and make himself manifest. So shall he sit in the temple of God"—as though to take God's place.

Twenty-two of the sermons of EDWIN SANDYS (1519-1588) have been preserved to our day. In his sermon on Isaiah 55:1: "Ho, every one that thirsteth, come ye to the waters...come ye, buy...without money and without price," he contrasted this invitation with that of the Papal Antichrist who requires money for his blessings: "He that sitteth in the temple of God, and termeth himself Christ's vicar, doth in like sort offer unto the people bread, water, wine, milk, pardon of sins, grace, mercy, and eternal life; but not freely: he is a merchant, he giveth nothing, and that is nothing which he selleth...his holy water cannot wash away the spots...his blasphemous masses do not appease, but provoke God's wrath...his rotten relics cannot comfort you...by his Latin service ye cannot be edified, or made wiser. Yet this trumpery they sell for money, and upon this trash they cause silly men to waste their substance....Thus you see a manifest difference between Christ and Antichrist."[86]

WILLIAM FLUKE (1538-1589), an English puritan, pointed to Rome as the seat of Antichrist (which was taken after the seat of the civil empire was removed) and that the Antichrist was a *succession* of men, not a single individual. By looking at Rome, he said, "It is easy to find the person by St. Paul's description; and this note especially, that excludeth the *heathen* tyrants, 'He shall sit in the temple of God': which we see to be fulfilled in the Pope...that 'Man of Sin,' and 'Son of Perdition,' the adversary that lifteth up himself 'above all that is called God'; and shall be destroyed 'by the glory of his coming'."[87]

SIR ISAAC NEWTON (1642-1727) is well known because of his scientific research, especially in connection with the laws of gravitation. He was a writer, mathematician, philosopher, and also a student of Bible prophecy! His *Observations Upon the Prophecies of Daniel and the Apocalypse of St. John*, was published six years after his death. Newton linked the little horn of Daniel 7 with the Papacy, rising among the ten kingdoms into which the Roman empire fell. "But it was a kingdom of a different kind from the other ten kingdoms....By its eyes it was a Seer; and by its mouth speaking great things and changing times and laws, it was a Prophet as well as a King. And such a Seer, a Prophet and a King, is the church of Rome. A Seer...is a Bishop in the literal sense of the word; and this church claims the universal Bishopric. With his mouth he gives laws to kings and nations as an Oracle; and pretends to Infallibility, and that his dictates are binding to the whole world; which is to be a Prophet in the highest degree."[88]

JOHANN ALBRECHT BENGEL (1687-1725) early became convinced that the Pope was the predicted Antichrist. Through his books which were translated into many languages, he had a strong influence upon a number of people, including Wesley.

167

JOHN WESLEY (1703-1791), founder of Methodism, whose ministry has affected the lives of multiplied thousands, believed the prophecies regarding the Antichrist, the man of sin, had found fulfillment in the "Romish Papacy."[89] In 1754, Wesley wrote these words concerning the Papacy: "He is in an emphatical sense, the Man of Sin, as he increases all manner of sin above

measure. And he is, too, properly styled the Son of Perdition, as he has caused the death of numberless multitudes, both of his opposers and followers....He it is...that exalteth himself above all that is called God, or that is worshipped...claiming the highest power, and highest honor...claiming the prerogatives which belong to God alone."[90]

Froom sums up the evidence in these words: "We have seen the remarkable unanimity of belief of Reformation leaders in every land that the Antichrist of prophecy is not to be a single individual—some sort of superman—who will wrack and well-nigh wreck the world just before the second advent of Christ. Instead, they found that it was a vast *system* of apostasy, or rather, an imposing counterfeit of truth which had developed within the jurisdiction of that divinely appointed custodian of truth, the Christian Church."[91]

A number of notable books on the Papal Antichrist were written during the centuries that followed the Reformation. We will mention two: *Roman Antichrist*, written in 1612 by Andreas Helwig of Berlin (the first, according to Froom as well as Elliott, to link the number 666 with the Papal designation "Vicarius Filii Dei"); and *Dissertations on the Prophecies*, written by Thomas Newton in 1748 which showed that the prophecy of the man of sin had found fulfillment in the Roman Papacy.

This same point was emphasized in the Protestant creeds. The *Westminster Confession of Faith* used by the Church of England, and later by the Presbyterian Church, says (Chapter 25, Section 6):

There is no other Head of the Church but the Lord Jesus Christ, nor can the Pope of Rome, in any sense, be head thereof, but is that Antichrist, that man of sin, and Son of Perdition, that exalteth himself in the Church, against Christ and all that is called God.

This same basic statement is found in *The Savoy Declaration* of the Congregational Church, the *Baptist Confession* of 1689, and in *The Philadelphia Confession of Faith*. The *Morland Confession* of 1508 and 1535 (which represented the beliefs of the Waldensian Brethren) says in article 8:

That Antichrist, that man of sin, doth sit in the temple of God, that is, in the church, of whom the prophets, and Christ and his apostles foretold, admonishing all the godly, to beware of him and his errors, and not suffer themselves to be drawn aside from the truth.

The Reformation work in Switzerland produced the *Helvetic Confession* in 1536 in which the Papacy is mentioned as the predicted Antichrist. The Lutheran statement contained in the *Smalcald Articles* says:

The Pope is the very Antichrist, who exalteth himself above, and opposeth himself against Christ, because he will not permit Christians to be saved without his power, which, nevertheless, is nothing, and is neither ordained nor commanded by God.

As Protestant churches were established in America, it was this same view concerning the Papacy that was held. In 1680 the churches of New England drew up a confession of faith which stated that Jesus Christ is the head of the church and *not* the Pope of Rome who is indeed *Antichrist*. "This," writes Froom, "was the commonly accepted American position."[92] As Samuel Lee (1625-1691), a learned minister of New Bristol, Rhode Island, said: "It is agreed among *all* maintainers of the Evangelical Church that the Roman Pontiff is Antichrist."[93]

ROGER WILLIAMS (1603-1683), founder of Rhode Island and pastor of the first Baptist church in America, spoke of the Pope as "the pretended Vicar of Christ on earth, who sits as God over the temple of God, exalting himself not only above all that is called God, but over the souls and consciences of all his vassals, yea over the Spirit of Christ, over the Holy Spirit, yea, and God himself...speaking against the God of heaven, thinking to change times and laws: but he is the son of perdition (2 Thessalonians 2)."[94]

COTTON MATHER (1663-1728), in his book, *Fall of Babylon*, asked the question: "Is the Pope of Rome to be looked upon as The Antichrist, whose coming and reigning was foretold in the ancient oracles?" To this he answered: "The oracles of God foretold the rising of an *Antichrist* in the Christian church; and in the Pope of Rome, *all* the characteristics of that Antichrist are so marvelously answered that if any who read the scriptures do not see it, there is a marvelous blindness upon them."[95]

SAMUEL COOPER (1725-1783), while delivering a series of lectures at Harvard, said: "If Antichrist is not to be found in the chair of St. Peter, he is nowhere to be found." He believed the Antichrist was the succession of bishops in Rome.[96]

JONATHAN EDWARDS (1703-1758), a famous revivalist and third president of Princeton, identified the "Pope and his clergy" as the power prophesied in 2 Thessalonians 2 and other places. His grandson, TIMOTHY DWIGHT (1752-1817), also a minister, spoke of how the Popes "have seated themselves in the church, or temple of God, and shewed that they were God, by assuming powers, which belong only to God: the powers, for instance, of making laws to bind the consciences of men; or pardoning sin; of forming religious establishments; of introducing new laws for the conduct and government of the church...thus have they exalted themselves above all that is called God, or that is worshipped."[97]

After many pages of carefully documented proof for his statement, Froom concludes: "The *futurist* view of an *individual* Antichrist was unknown among the Protestants of North America prior to the nineteenth century"![98] Today, however, there are many Christians who have only heard the futurist ideas. They are not even aware that another interpretation exists!

There were *two* great truths that stood out in the preaching that brought about the Protestant Reformation: (1) The just shall live by faith (not by works of Romanism);

and (2) the Papacy is the Antichrist of scripture. It was a message FOR Christ and AGAINST Antichrist! Says Froom, "The entire Reformation rested on this twofold testimony."[99]

Hundreds of books were written in the contest of Protestant and Catholic pens regarding Antichrist. So great was the stir, in 1516 the Fifth Lateran Council rose up forbidding anyone to write or preach on the subject of Antichrist. Nevertheless, in Germany, Switzerland, England, France, Denmark, and Sweden, the message continued with power and conviction by the ministers of the various Protestant churches. The scriptures were getting into the hands of the people. Thousands had come to recognize the Papacy as the Antichrist—a teaching which dealt havoc to the church of Rome.

THE COUNTER INTERPRETATION

The Roman Catholic church saw that it must produce a counter interpretation or lose the battle. As the *Encyclopedia Britannica* says: "Under the stress of the Protestant attack there arose new methods on the papal side," special mention being made of the Jesuit Ribera, the founder of the futurist school of interpretation.[100]

Francisco Ribera (1537-1591) published a 500 page commentary on the grand points of Babylon and Antichrist, the object being to set aside the Protestant teaching that the Papacy is the Antichrist. In his commentary, he assigned the first chapters of Revelation to the first century. The rest he restricted to a literal three and a half years at the end of time. He taught that the Jewish temple would be rebuilt by a single, individual Antichrist who would abolish the Christian reli-

PHOTO OF THE TITLE PAGE OF THE JESUIT RIBERA'S FUTURIST COMMENTARY OF THE APOCALYPSE, DATED 1591, A.D. SALAMANCA.

gion, deny Christ, pretend to be God, and conquer the world. When Thomas Brightman (1562-1607), a Protestant scholar and reformer, first saw a copy of Ribera's futurist exposition, he was aroused to indignation. "Once they would not suffer any man to scarce touch a Bible, now they produce a commentary to explain it—to point men away from the Papal Antichrist."

For two more centuries the futurist view regarding Antichrist was rejected by the Protestant church. Then in 1826, Samuel R. Maitland (1792-1866), librarian to the Archbishop of Canterbury, became the first Protestant to accept Ribera's futurist interpretation. Says Ladd: "This futurist interpretation with its personal Antichrist and three and a half year tribulation did not take root in the Protestant church until the early nineteenth century. The first Protestant to adopt it was S.R. Maitland."[101]

Froom sums it up in these words:

In Ribera's Commentary was laid the foundation for that great structure of Futurism, built upon and enlarged by those who followed, until it became the common Catholic position. And then, wonder of wonders, in the nineteenth century this Jesuit scheme of interpretation came to be adopted by a growing number of Protestants, until today Futurism, amplified and adorned with the rapture theory, has become the generally accepted belief of the Fundamentalist wing of popular Protestantism![102]

Because of the flood of futurist prophecy books that are widely circulated today, there is much speculation as to whether this world leader or that will soon emerge as the Antichrist of Bible prophecy. Many Christians are unaware of the old, standard, Protestant interpretation of the Reformers; that the man of sin rose to power following the breakup of the Roman empire; that he seated himself above all others in the church of the falling away; that these things have found fulfillment in the Papacy.

Today the Pope has world-wide fame. Multiplied thousands attend masses he performs. His travels and activities are given far-reaching news coverage. He is visited by presidents and kings. In the eyes of many, he is a man of peace and good will. Millions of Roman Catholics look to him as the *head* of the church, a belief that is foundational to the entire structure of Roman Catholicism. All of this raises one basic question that should not be lightly brushed aside: *Is the Pope the head of the church?*

If the Pope *is* the head of the church, then Protestants surely err by not acknowledging him as such. But if he is *not*, what can be said about a system that makes such a claim? The Reformers taught that the head of the church is CHRIST and that the Papacy is Antichrist. For this position there are strong Biblical and historical arguments, as we have shared here. Some will see this as "the" fulfillment of the prophecies regarding Antichrist; others will see it as "a" fulfillment, not ruling out some final fulfillment. But in any event, we do not believe a true understanding can be obtained by speculating about the future, while ignoring so much in the past.

* * * * * * * * * * *

Now you have read the book. Some have rejoiced in the understanding it has given on Bible prophecy. Others have disagreed with it. Clearly there are sharp differences between the futurist and fulfilled viewpoints. But look at it this way: Christians on one side believe Jesus is coming, and much Bible prophecy is about to be fulfilled; other Christians believe Jesus is coming because much Bible prophecy has *already been fulfilled.* In either case, they share a *common ground:* FAITH IN JESUS CHRIST! And so, we would emphasize, these things have been presented "for the *edifying* of the body of Christ"—not for strife or division—so that by "speaking the truth in *love,* we may grow up into him in all things, which is the head, even Christ" (Ephesians 4:12-15).

Having seen how the prophecies about wars, famines, earthquakes, the spread of the gospel, the abomination of desolation, the fall of Jerusalem, the tribulation, the seventy weeks, the time of Jacob's trouble, the falling away, and the rise of the man of sin have been fulfilled, surely with joyful expectation we can look forward to the fulfillment of that glad day when he shall come who *is:*

THE KING OF KINGS AND LORD OF LORDS!

NOTES

INTRODUCTION

1. M.R. De Haan, *Thirty-five Simple Studies on the Major Themes in Revelation* (Grand Rapids: Zondervan, 1946), p.111.

2. Oswald J. Smith, *Tribulation or Rapture—Which?* (London: The Sovereign Grace Advent Testimony), pp.3,10.

3. Finis Jennings Dake, *Dake's Annotated Reference Bible* (Atlanta: Dake Bible Sales, Inc., 1963), p.227.

4. George B. Fletcher, *Will the Second Coming of Christ be in Two Stages?*, p.2.

5. Herschel W. Ford, *Seven Simple Sermons on the Second Coming* (Grand Rapids: Zondervan, 1946), p.44.

6. Fred J. Peters, *The Mystery of Antichrist* (Blackwood, NJ: Old Fashioned Prophecy Magazine, reprint of 1942 edition), p.50.

7. C.I. Scofield, *Scofield Reference Bible* (New York: Oxford University Press, 1917), p.914.

8. Philip Mauro, *The Seventy Weeks and the Great Tribulation* (Swengel, PA.: Reiner Publications, 1944 edition), p.80.

PART ONE: WILL THE RETURN OF CHRIST BE IN TWO STAGES?

1. Oral Roberts, *How to be Personally Prepared for the Second Coming of Christ* (Tulsa: Oral Roberts Evangelistic Association, 1967), p.34.

2. Jesse F. Silver, *The Lord's Return* (New York: Revell, 1914), p.260.

3. Herschel W. Ford, *Seven Simple Sermons on the Second Coming* (Grand Rapids: Zondervan, 1946), p.51.

4. Hal Lindsey, *The Late Great Planet Earth* (Grand Rapids: Zondervan Publishing House, 1970), p.143.

5. G.S. Bishop, *The Doctrine of Grace*, p.341.

6. C.I. Scofield, *Scofield Reference Bible* (New York: Oxford University Press, 1917), p.1016.

7. Hal Lindsey, *op. cit.,* p.111.

8. Frank M. Boyd, *Ages and Dispensations* (Springfield: Gospel Publishing House, 1955), p.60.

9. William W. Orr, *Antichrist, Armageddon, and the End of the World* (Grand Rapids: Dunham Publishing Company, 1966), p.9.

10. Carl Sabiers, *Where Are the Dead?*, pp.123,124.

11. Oswald Smith, *Tribulation or Rapture—Which?* (London: The Sovereign Grace Advent Testimony), p.9.

12. *The Pulpit Commentary* (Grand Rapids: Eerdmans Publishing Company, reprint 1950), Vol.22, p.12.

13. *Ibid.,* Vol. 3, p.534.

14. Matthew Henry, *Matthew Henry's Commentary* (New York: Fleming H. Revell Company, reprint of 1721 edition), p.874. Cf. Job 15:15; Psalms 89:5,7; Daniel 8:13; 4:13.

15. Oswald Smith, *op. cit.,* p.10.

16. William R. Kimball, *The Rapture, A Question of Timing* (Grand Rapids: Baker Book House, 1985), p.179, quoted from *Christianity Today,* August 1959.

17. Pat Robertson, *Answers to 200 of Life's Most Probing Questions* (Nashville: Thomas Nelson Publishers, 1984), pp.155,156.

18. Wilfrid C. "Will" Meloon, *Eschaton,* issue XVI (Orange City, FL: 1979).

19. Scofield, *op. cit.,* p.1334.

20. M.R. De Haan, *Thirty-five Simple Studies on the Major Themes in Revelation* (Grand Rapids: Zondervan, 1946), p.61.

21. Scofield, *op. cit.,* p.1348.

22. *Ibid.,* p.1212.

23. George E. Ladd, *The Blessed Hope* (Grand Rapids: Eerdmans, 1956), p.31.

24. *Ibid.*

25. Barnabas, in *Ante-Nicene Fathers,* Vol. 1, pp. 146,138.

26. Justin, *Dialogue with Trypho*, chapter 52.

27. Irenaeus, *Against Heresies*, 35:1, 30:4, 26:1, 29:1.

28. Tertullian, *On the Resurrection of the Flesh*, chapter Twenty-two.

29. Hippolytus, *Treatise on Christ and Antichrist*, chapters 66,67.

30. Cyprian, *Epistle 55*.

31. Lactantius, *The Divine Institutes*, Vol.7.

32. *The Catechetical Lectures of St. Cyril*, Lecture 15.

33. Irenaeus, *op. cit.*, 5:29.

34. *Hermas*, Vision 4, chapter 2.

35. *Ibid.*, Vision 2, chapter 2.

36. LeRoy E. Froom, *The Prophetic Faith of Our Fathers* (Washington: Review and Herald, 1945), Vol.3, p.516.

37. John L. Bray, *The Origin of the Pre-Tribulation Rapture Teaching* (Lakeland, FL: John L. Bray Ministry, Inc., 1982).

38. Manuel de Lacunza, *The Coming of Messiah in Glory and Majesty* (London: translated by Irving, 1827), Vol.1, p.99.

39. Quoted by Dave MacPherson, *The Great Rapture Hoax* (Fletcher, NC: New Puritan Library, 1983), pp.125-128.

40. S.P. Tregelles, *The Hope of Christ's Second Coming* (London: Samuel Bagster and Sons, 1864), pp.34-37.

41. *Dr. C.I. Scofield's Question Box*, (Chicago: The Bible Institute Colportage Association, compiled by Ella E. Pohle), p.93.

42. Smith, *op. cit.*, pp.2,3.

43. Kimball, *op. cit.*, pp.177,178.

44. *Ibid.*

PART TWO: THE GREAT TRIBULATION

1. Matthew Henry, *Commentary on the Whole Bible* (New York: Fleming H. Revell Company, reprint), Vol.5, p.352.

2. Flavius Josephus, *Wars of the Jews* (Philadelphia: The John C. Winston Company, 1957 edition), 2, 15-19.

3. *Ibid.*, 19:5-8.

4. Thomas Newton, *Dissertations on the Prophecies* (London: 1754), p.389; also see Eusebius, *Ecclesiastical History*, Book 3, chapter 5; Alfred Edersheim, *The Life and Times of Jesus the Messiah* (Grand Rapids: 1968 edition), p.448.

5. Adam Clarke, *Clarke's Commentary* (Nashville: Abingdon Press, reprint), Vol.5, p.228.

6. Josephus, *op. cit.*, Book 3, 1:1-3; 4, 9-11.

7. Oral Roberts, *How to be Personally Prepared for the Second Coming of Christ* (Tulsa: Oral Roberts Evangelistic Association, 1967), p.38.

8. Richard W. De Haan, *The Antichrist and Armageddon* (Grand Rapids: Radio Bible Class, 1968), p.13. (booklet)

9. W.E. Blackstone, *Jesus is Coming* (New York: Fleming H. Revell Company, 1932 reprint), p.187.

10. Hal Lindsey, *The Late Great Planet Earth* (Grand Rapids: Zondervan, 1970), p.56.

11. *Ibid.*, p.153.

12. Charles Halff, *Will There be a War Between Russia and America?* (San Antonio, TX: The Christian Jew Hour), pp.32-35.

13. Josephus, *op. cit.*, 2, 18:2.

14. *Ibid.*, 2, 18:8.

15. *Ibid.*, 3, 4:1.

16. *Ibid.*, 2, 18:3.

17. *Ibid.*, 4, 5:3.

18. *Ibid.*, 5, 1:3.

19. *Ibid.*, 5, 1:5.

20. *Ibid.*, 5, 11:1,2.

21. *Ibid.*, 5, 12:3; 6, 1:1.

22. *Ibid.*, 5, 10:3.

23. *Ibid.*, 6, 3:4.

24. *Ibid.*, 5, 13:4.

25. *Ibid.*, 6, 5:1.

26. *Ibid.*, 6, 4:5.

27. *Ibid.*, 6, 8,9.

28. *Ibid.*, 6, 9:3,4.

29. *Ibid.*, 5, 10:5.

30. *Ibid.*, Preface.

31. Loraine Boettner, *The Millennium* (Philadelphia: Presbyterian and Reformed Publishing Company, 1957), p.202.

32. H.A. Ironside, *The Great Parenthesis* (Grand Rapids: Zondervan, 1945), p.94.

33. C.I. Scofield, *Scofield Reference Bible* (New York: Oxford University Press, 1917), p.1106.

34. J. Stuart Russell, *The Parousia* (Grand Rapids: Baker Book House, 1983, reprint of 1878 edition).

35. Josephus, *op. cit.*, 6, 5:3.

36. Lindsey, *op. cit.*, p.53,54.

37. Finnis Jennings Dake, *Dake's Annotated Reference Bible* (Atlanta: Dake Bible Sales, Inc., 1963), p.27.

38. C.I. Scofield, *op. cit.*, p.1032.

39. *Ibid.*, p.1034.

40. Howard Estep, *Rapture or Tribulation?* (Colton, CA: World Prophetic Ministry), p.15.

41. J.G. Hall, *Prophecy Marches On!* (Springfield, MO: 1964), p.66; Ironside, *op. cit.*, p.111, etc.

42. H. Grattan Guinness, *Light for the Last Days* (London: Hodder and Stoughton, 1893).

PART THREE: DANIEL'S SEVENTIETH WEEK

1. Humphrey Prideaux, *The Old and New Testament Connected in the History of the Jews* (New York: Harper and Brothers, 1842), Vol.1, p.137.

2. Flavius Josephus, *Antiquities of the Jews* (Philadelphia: The John C. Winston Company, 1957 edition), Book 11, 1:1,2.

3. Robert Anderson, *The Coming Prince* (1895), p.124.

4. Philip Mauro, *The Seventy Weeks and the Great Tribulation* (Swengel, PA: Reiner Publications, 1944 edition), pp.22,24.

5. C.I. Scofield, *What Do the Prophets Say?* (Philadelphia: The Sunday School Times, 1916), p.142.

6. A.C. Gaebelein, *The Prophet Daniel* (1911), pp. 134,135.

7. Edward J. Young, *The Prophecy of Daniel—A Commentary* (Grand Rapids: Eerdmans Publishing Company, 1949), p.203.

8. Josephus, *op. cit.*, Book 11, 1:2,3.

9. *Ibid.*

10. Oliver Greene, *Daniel—Verse by Verse Study* (1964), p.365.

11. Eusebius, *The Proof of the Gospel*, Book 8, chapter 2.

12. Quoted by LeRoy Froom in *The Prophetic Faith of Our Fathers* (Washington: Review and Herald, 1945), Vol.1, p.487.

13. Adam Clarke, *Clarke's Commentary* (Nashville: Abingdon Press, reprint), Vol.4, p.602.

14. H.A. Ironside, *The Great Parenthesis* (Grand Rapids: Zondervan, 1945), P.50.

15. Richard De Haan, *The Antichrist and Armageddon* (Grand Rapids: Radio Bible Class, 1968).

16. W. Kelly, *Daniel's Seventy Weeks* (New York: Loizeaux), p.18.

17. H. Grattan Guinness, *The Approaching End of the Age* (London: Hodder and Stoughton, 1879), p.712.

18. William Orr, *Antichrist, Armageddon, and the End of the World* (Grand Rapids: Dunham Publishing Company, 1966), pp.22-23. (booklet).

19. John R. Rice, *The Coming Kingdom of Christ* (Wheaton, IL: Sword of the Lord Publishers, 1945), p.123.

20. Howard Estep, *Jacob's Trouble* (Colton, CA: World Prophetic Ministry), p.26. (booklet)

21. Frank M. Boyd, *Ages and Dispensations* (Springfield, MO: Gospel Publishing House, 1955), p.69.

22. Finnis Jennings Dake, *Dake's Annotated Reference Bible* (Atlanta: Dake Bible Sales, Inc., 1963), p.230.

23. Hal Lindsey, *The Late Great Planet Earth* (Grand Rapids: Zondervan, 1970), p.57.

24. Greene, *op. cit.*, pp.387,388; J.G. Hall, *Prophecy Marches On!*, p.58; Boyd, *op. cit.*, p.69; Dake, *op. cit.*, p.868; etc.

25. W. Kelly, *op. cit.*, p.19, etc.

26. Clarence H. Hewitt, *The Seer of Babylon—Studies in the Book of Daniel* (Boston: Advent Christian Publication Society, 1948), p.258.

27. Dake, *op. cit.*, p.877, etc.

28. Ironside, *op. cit.*, p.23.

29. George L. Murray, *Millennial Studies* (Grand Rapids: Eerdmans, 1948), p.104,105.

30. Kelly, *op. cit.*, pp.17,20.

31. Albert Barnes, *Barnes' Notes on Daniel* (1881), p.372.

32. John Peter Lange, *Lange Commentary*, Volume 13 (New York: Charles Scribner's Sons, 1884), p.188.

33. Froom, *op. cit.*, Vol. 1, p.278.

34. Hippolytus, *Treatise on Christ and Antichrist*, chapters 66,67.

35. Zephaniah 1:17; 2:5-13; Nahum 1:1,2; 2:13; 3:5-7; Amos 1:7-15; 2:2,3; Jeremiah 49:27; Micah 1:6,7; 5:10-14; Ezekiel 28:22.

36. Jeremiah 44:6; 52:12-14; 2 Chronicles 36:14-19; Hosea 8:14; Ezekiel 15:7,8; Zephaniah 1:4,12.

PART FOUR: THE ANTICHRIST

1. John R. Rice, *World-wide War and the Bible*, p.212.

2. M.R. De Haan, *Thirty-five Simple Studies on the Major Themes in Revelation* (Grand Rapids: Zondervan, 1946), p.184.

3. Dan Gilbert, *Who Will be the Antichrist?*, p.21.

4. Oral Roberts, *How to be Personally Prepared for the Second Coming of Christ* (Tulsa: Oral Roberts Evangelistic Association, 1967), p.36.

5. Baron Alfred Porcelli, *The Antichrist—His Portrait and History* (Blackwood, NJ: Old Fashioned Prophecy Magazine, 1971, reprint of 1943 edition), p.49.

6. LeRoy E. Froom, *The Prophetic Faith of Our Fathers* (Washington: Review and Herald, 1945), Vol.1, p.19.

7. *Ibid.*, p.271.

8. *Ibid.*, p.258.

9. Thomas Newton, *Dissertations on the Prophecies* (London: 1754), p.463.

10. Jerome, *Commentaria*, Book 5, chapter 25.

11. Porcelli, *op. cit.*, p.49.

12. Newton, *op. cit.*, p.463.

13. Chrysostom, *Homilies*, pp.388,389.

14. Edward B. Elliott, *Horae Apocalyticae* (London: Seeley, Burnside, and Seeley, 1846), Book 3, p.92.

15. Denny, *Commentary on Thessalonians*, p.325.

16. Froom, *op. cit.*, Vol.1, p.150.

17. H. Grattan Guinness, *Romanism and the Reformation* (Blackwood, NJ: Old Fashioned Prophecy Magazine, 1967—reprint of 1887 edition), p.119.

18. Adam Clarke, *Clarke's Commentary* (Nashville: Abingdon Press), Vol.6, p.569.

19. *Encyclopedia Britannica* (1961 edition, article: "Antichrist"), Vol.2, p.60.

20. Jerome, *op. cit.*, Book 5, chapter 25.

21. Chrysostom, *Homilies*, p.388,389.

22. Albert Barnes, *Barnes' Commentary*, p.1115.

23. Alexander Flick, *The Rise of the Medieval Church* (New York: G.P. Putnam's Sons, 1908, reprint 1959), p.168.

24. Quoted by Clarence H. Hewitt in *The Seer of Babylon*, p.113.

25. Guinness, *op. cit.*, p.61.

26. William W. Orr, *Antichrist, Armageddon, and the End of the World* (Grand Rapids: Dunham Publishing Company, 1966), p.11. (booklet)

27. John R. Rice, *The Coming Kingdom of Christ* (Wheaton, IL: Sword of the Lord Publishers, 1945), p.125.

28. Scofield, *Scofield Reference Bible* (New York, Oxford University Press, 1917), p.1272.

29. Oswald J. Smith, *Tribulation or Rapture—Which?* (London: The Sovereign Grace Advent Testimony), p.8.

30. Hogg and Vine, *The Epistle to the Thessalonians*.

31. Hyman Appleman, *Antichrist and the Jews* (Grand Rapids: Zondervan, 1950), p.12. (booklet).

32. Hal Lindsey, *The Late Great Planet Earth* (Grand Rapids: Zondervan, 1970), p.111.

33. Elliott, *op. cit.*, Vol.3, p.139.

34. Guinness, *op. cit.*, p.28.

35. M.R. De Haan, *Will the Church Go Through the Tribulation?* (Grand Rapids: Radio Bible Class), p.25.

36. R.C.H. Lenski, *The Interpretation of St. Paul's Epistles*, p.433.

37. Ralph Woodrow, *Babylon Mystery Religion* (Riverside, CA: Ralph Woodrow Evangelistic Association, Inc., 1966).

38. Newton, *op. cit.*

39. Barnes, *op. cit.*, p.1112.

40. *Ibid.*, p.1114.

41. Guinness, *op. cit.*, p.57.

42. Barnes, *op. cit.*, p.1114.

43. See John Foxe, *Acts and Monuments.*

44. Scofield, *op. cit.*, p.1322.

45. *Ibid.*, p.918.

46. Howard C. Estep, *Antichrist's Kingdom* (Colton, CA: World Prophetic Ministry), p.24. (booklet)

47. V.K. Van De Venter, *Some Errors of Futurism* (booklet, 1936) quoting Maitland, p.8.

48. Guinness, *op. cit.*, p.125.

49. Fred Peters, *op. cit.*, p.29.

50. Elliott, *op. cit.*, Vol.1, pp.67,68.

51. Porcelli, *op. cit.*, p.72.

52. Froom, *op. cit.*, Vol.2, p.66.

53. *Ibid.*, Vol.1, p.798.

54. Foxe, *op. cit.*, p.445.

55. Froom, *op. cit.*, Vol.2,p.55.

56. Guinness, *op. cit.*, p.134.

57. Foxe, *op. cit.*, Vol.1, p.543.

58. *Ibid.*, pp.636-641.

59. Froom, *op. cit.*, Vol.2, p.121.

60. *Ibid.*, p.116.

61. *Ibid.*, p.256.

62. Martin Luther, *First Principles*, pp.196,197.

63. Froom, *op. cit.*, Vol.2, p.281.

64. Luther, *Works*, Vol.2, p.385.

65. *Encyclopedia Britannica*, Article: "Antichrist," Vol.2, p.61.

66. Froom, *op. cit.*, Vol.2, p.296,299.

67. *Ibid.*, p.305.

68. *Ibid.*, p.288.

69. Calvin, *Tracts*, Vol.1, pp.219,220.

70. Knox, *The Zurich Letters*, p.199.

71. *Principal Works of Zwingli*, Vol.7, p.135.

72. Froom, *op. cit.*, Vol.2, pp.343,344.

73. Bibliander, *Relation Fidelis*, p.58.

74. Froom, *op. cit.*, Vol.2, p.319.

75. *Ibid.*, p.461.

76. *Ibid.*, p.356.

77. *Ibid.*, pp.540,541.

78. *Letters of Bishop Ridley*, Letter 32.

79. Froom, *op. cit.*, Vol.2, pp.377,379.

80. Cranmer, *Works*, Vol.1, pp.6,7.

81. *Ibid.*, pp.62,63.

82. Froom, *op. cit.*, Vol.2, pp.381,382.

83. *Ibid.*, p.403.

84. *Ibid.*, p.371.

85. Jewel, *An Exposition Upon the Two Epistles to the Thessalonians*, Vol.2, p.813.

86. *The Sermons of Edwin Sandys*, pp.11,12.

87. Froom, *op. cit.*

88. Sir Isaac Newton, *Observations Upon the Prophecies* (London: 1831 edition), p.75.

89. Wesley, *Explanatory Notes Upon the New Testament*, pp.290.

90. Quoted by Albert Close, *Antichrist and His Ten Kingdoms* (London: Thynne and Company, 1917), p.110.

91. Froom, *op. cit.*, Vol.2, p.793.

92. *Ibid.*, Vol.3, p.111.

93. Lee, *The Cutting Off of Antichrist*, p.1.

94. Froom, *op. cit.*, Vol.3, p.52.

95. *Ibid.*, Vol.3, p.113.

96. Cooper, *A Discourse on the Man of Sin*, p.12.

97. Dwight, *A sermon Preached at Northampton*, p.27.

98. Froom, *op. cit.*, Vol.3, p.257.

99. *Ibid.*, Vol.2, p.243.

100. *Encyclopedia Britannica,* (New York: Encyclopedia Britannica, Inc., 1910), Eleventh edition, Vol.23, p.213.

101. George Ladd, *The Blessed Hope* (Grand Rapids: Eerdmans, 1956), p.38.

102. Froom, *op. cit.*, Vol.2, p.493.

All scriptures in the Bible that teach the second coming of Christ will be in two stages are listed below: